LIFE FORMS

LIFE FORMS

Photographing Metaphor

BARRY SHEINKOPF

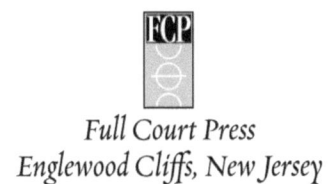

Full Court Press
Englewood Cliffs, New Jersey

First Edition

Copyright © 2012 by Barry Sheinkopf

Published in the United States of America
by Full Court Press, 601 Palisade Avenue
Englewood Cliffs, NJ 07632

ISBN 978-0-970-94774-1
Library of Congress Control No. 2012931549

Editing and Book Design by Barry Sheinkopf for Bookshapers
(www.bookshapers.com)
Author Photo by David Sheinkopf
Cover Image,"Red Cabbage," 1977
Colophon by Liz Sedlack

FOR FRAN,
who reminded me

AND FOR EUGENIA,
AND DAVID AND SUSAN,
who know them best

A Note

Books of photographs don't need prefaces, but writers chronically seem to depend on them, so I ask your indulgence for a few words about the images to follow.

I wrote, in partial defense of the thinness of my *Collected Poems* (Full Court, 2009—a volume of barely two hundred pages that represented forty years of work), that "there would be more of them if I hadn't got it into my head at one point to write poems that were so short they contained no words at all, and been thus drawn to the still camera." My aim in shooting these pictures has been from the start to photograph metaphors—to momentarily puzzle the eye, which knows that it must be looking at the real world but can't quite recognize it, by reaching visually for something other than the mere facts of reality.

I have tried to do so with an absence of technical trickery. I believe, with Ansel Adams, in the necessity of wholly capturing an image in the viewfinder *before the shutter is tripped*. I point this out because photography has been so vastly transformed during my lifetime. As a result, my photographs have taken the journey from film to digital with various jolts and bumps along the way.

In some respects, it's been a iffy trip. That we are at the zenith of technological ease in making and refining color photographs is hardly news—automatic exposure programs on digital SLRs are far more sophisticated than they've ever been, and Photoshop, with a few clicks, can camouflage a host of photographic flaws. This potential, though, often blinds photographers to the necessity of seeing, because the seeing can never be added later by Photoshop or any other program, and the result of trying to do so will always be a photograph that fails to speak to a viewer. I use Photoshop to interpret RAW images in the same way I once used to use an enlarger to interpret black-and-white negatives, but I do so sparingly. My wife, bless her, views *all* Photoshop interventions with a gimlet eye, as well she may. I plead in my defense that I have removed flaws from images only when I never wanted them in the first place (especially those I made to the digital versions of 25 ASA transparencies, like the dust particles on my *Tomato,* which I thought were a distraction when I originally made the image but couldn't remove them, and which, I'm happy to report, are now gone).

In the end, that is to say, the camera ought to be a transparent bridge between me and you. Otherwise, the glory of the many forms life takes is diminished.

I made all these images with Nikkormat FTN film and Nikon digital cameras, fixed-focus Nikon lenses of various focal lengths, and two generations of Nikon macro lenses, with the camera mounted on a good tripod (the Leitz Tilt-all, and, later, a Slik carbon-fiber model, neither of which exhibited camera moment). I've commonly used polarizing filters, and less commonly an assortment of others—neutral density, color compensation, and so forth.

Titles and other accompanying information about each photograph are to be found at the back of this book.

—B.S., West New York, 2011

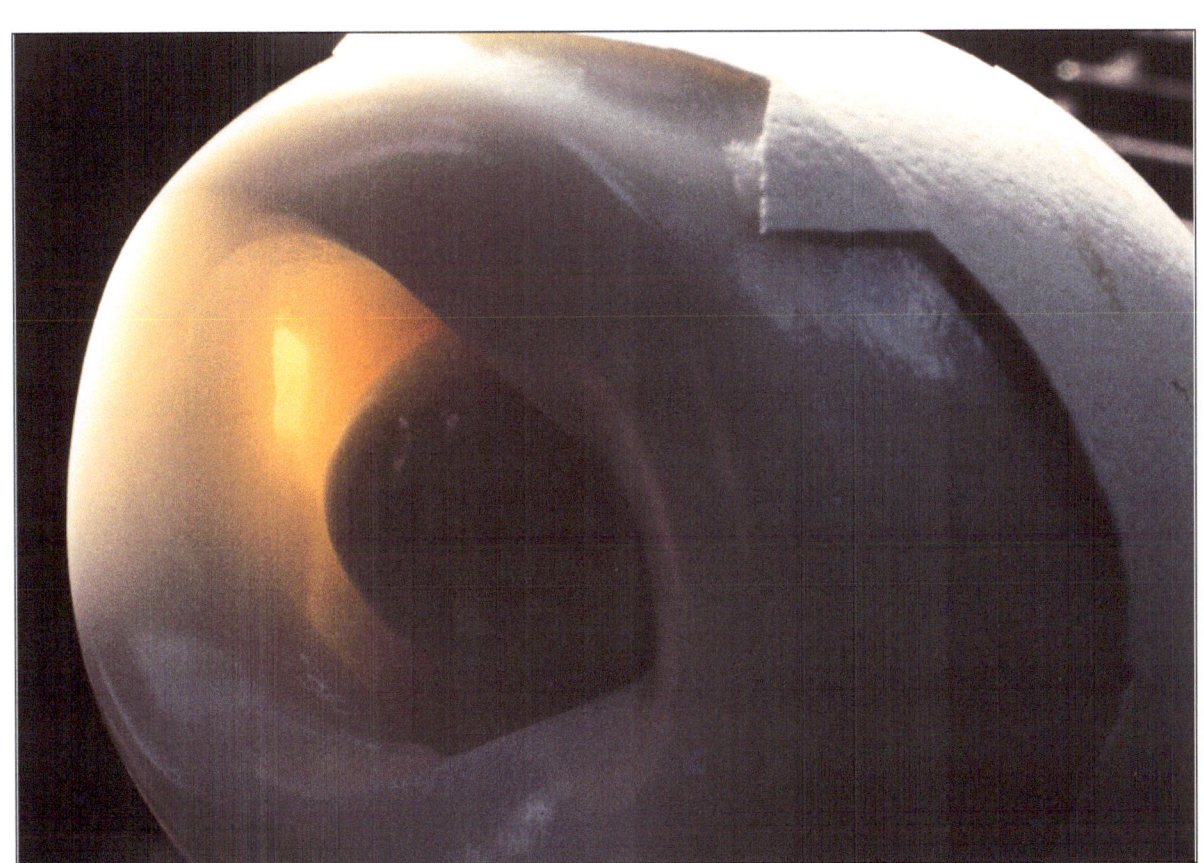

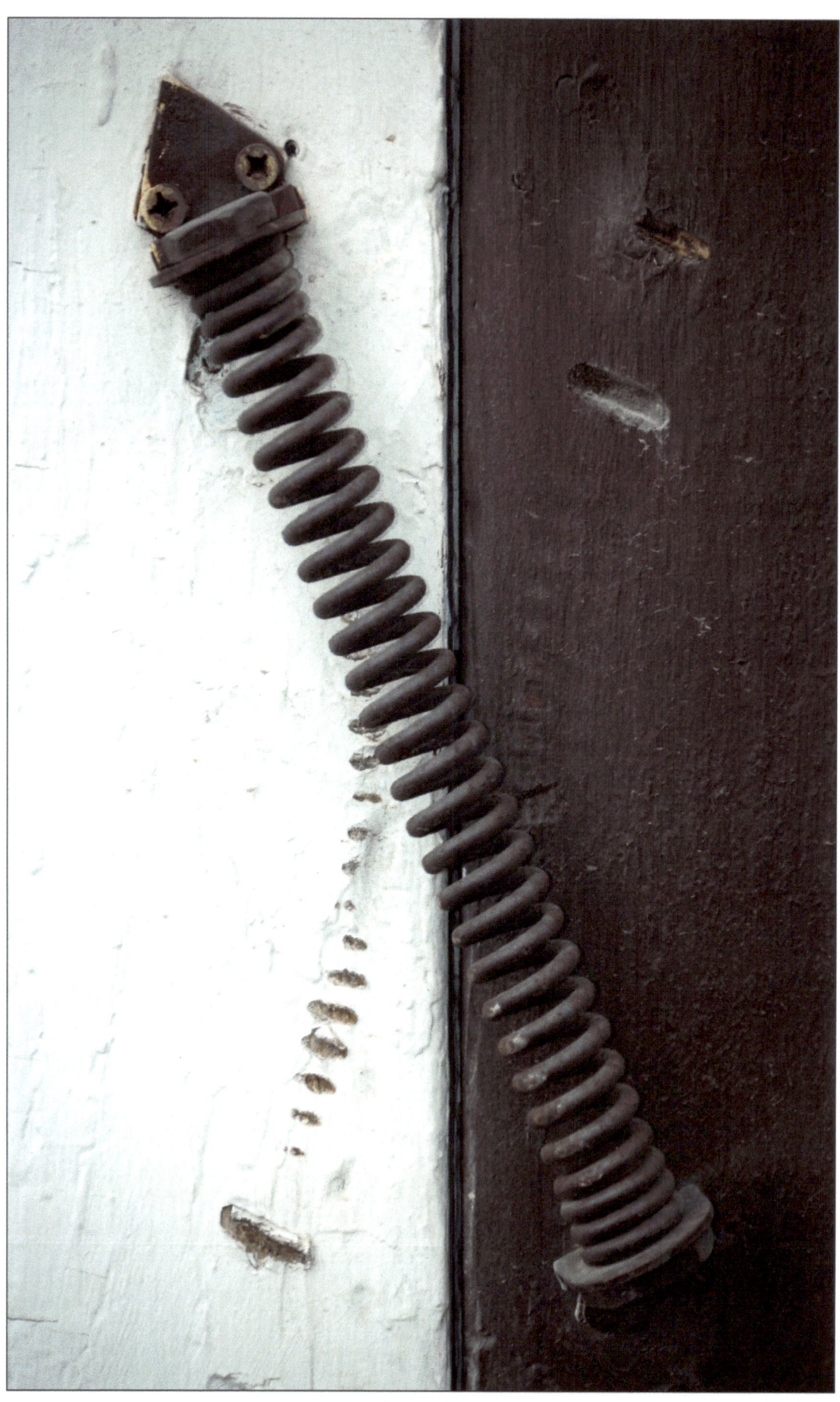

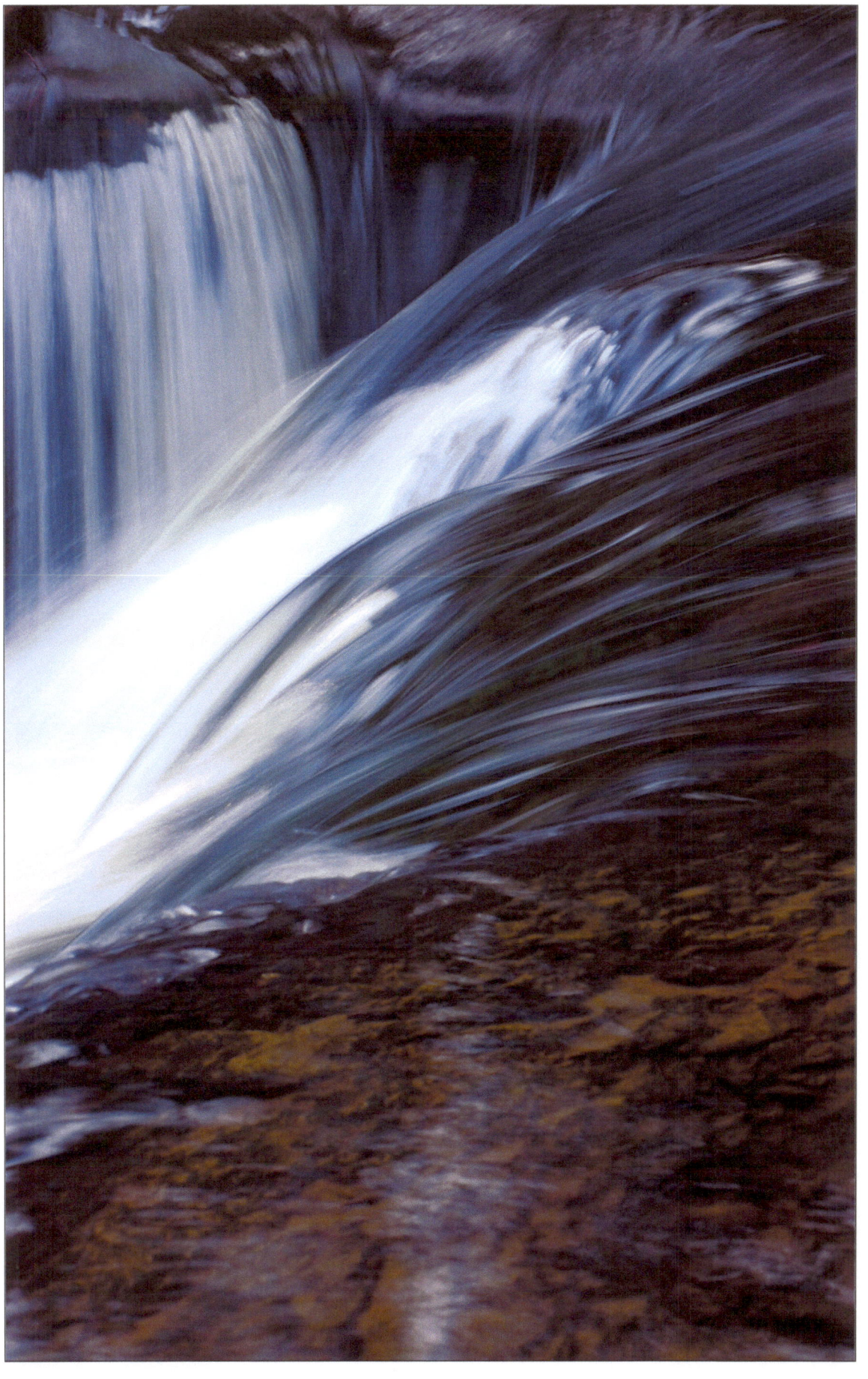

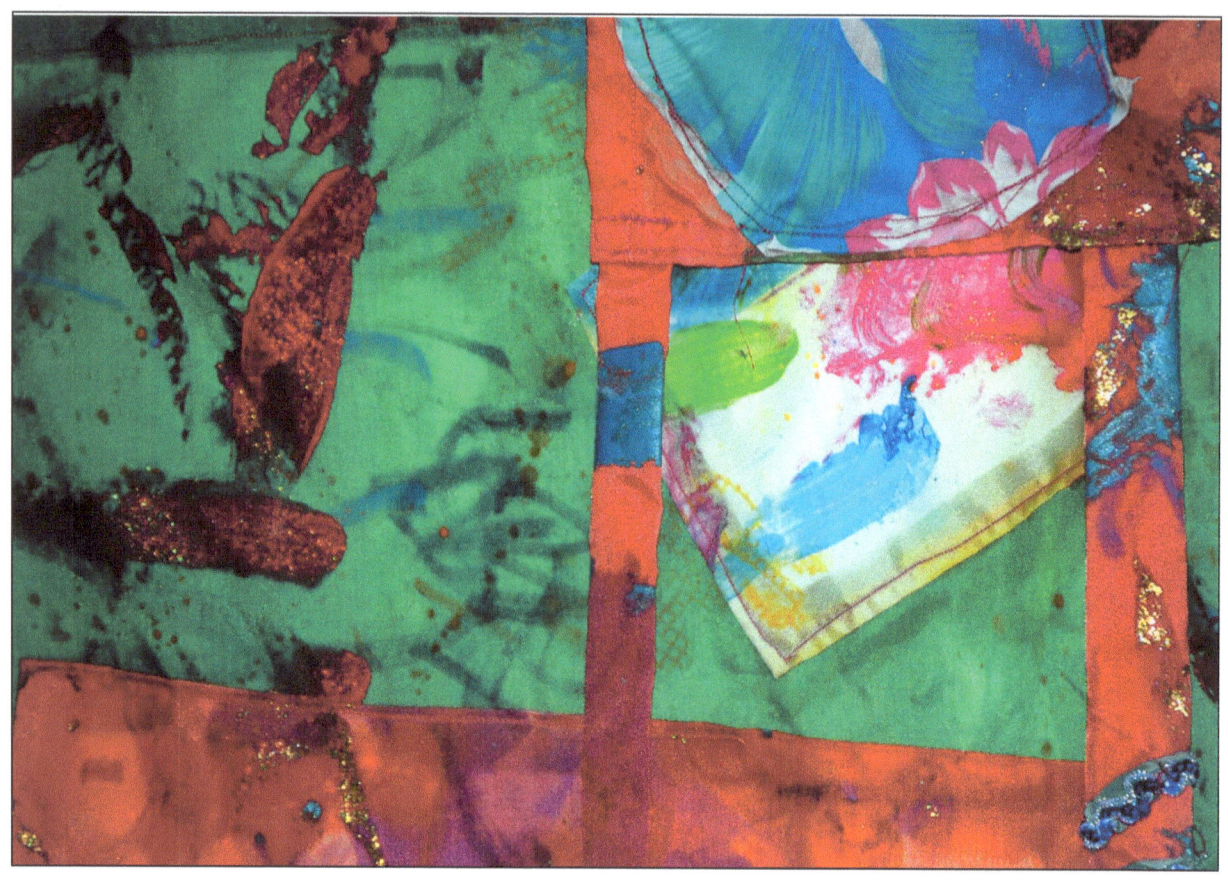

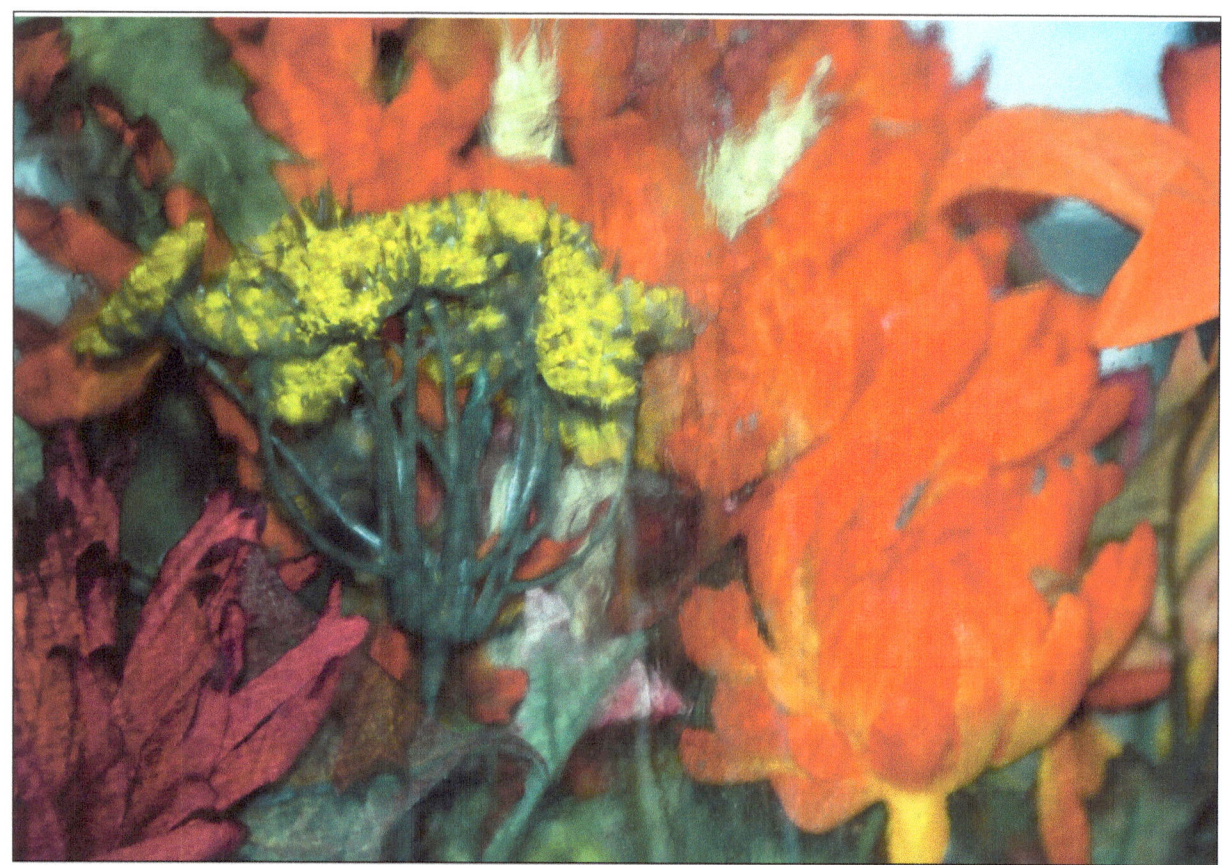

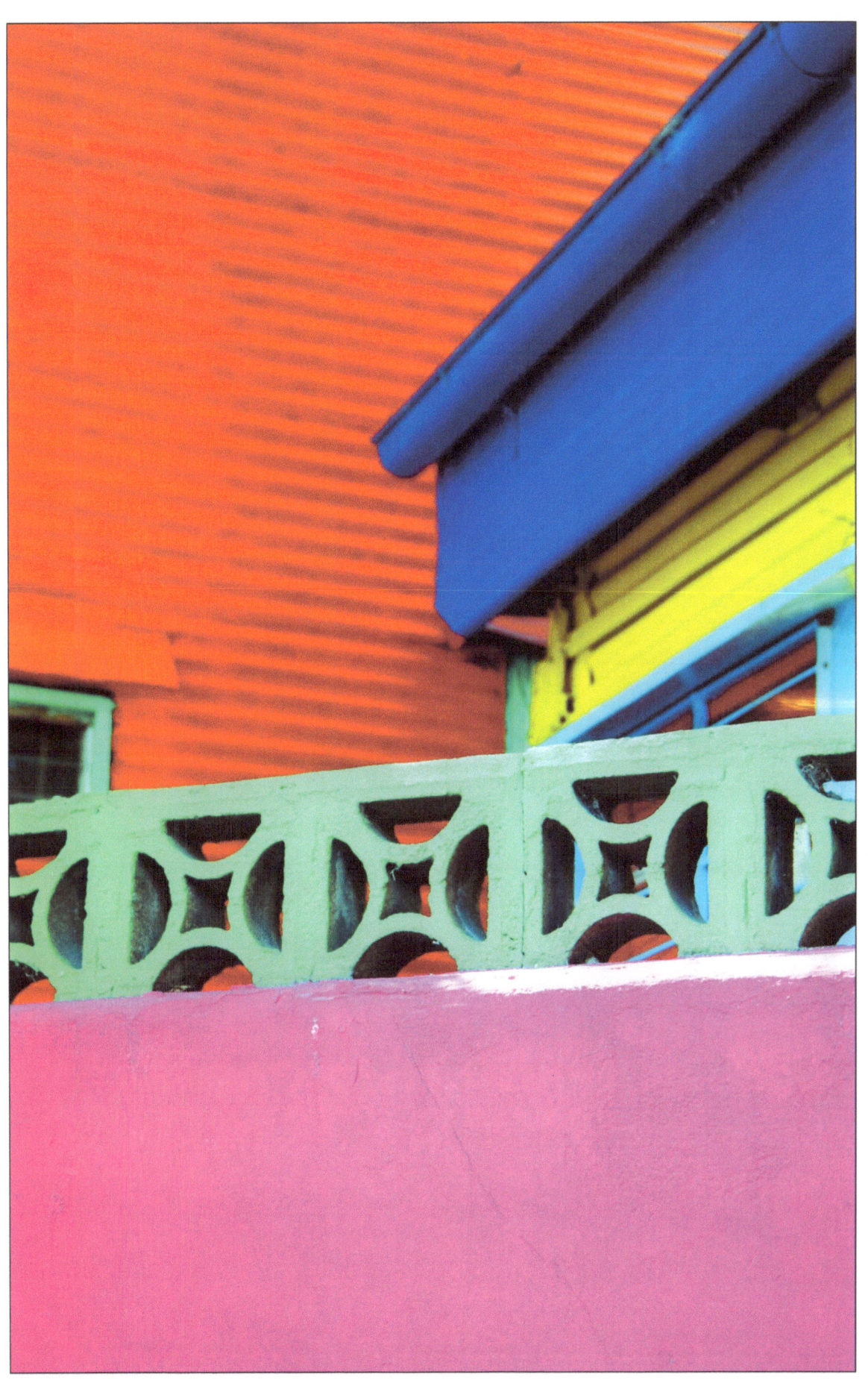

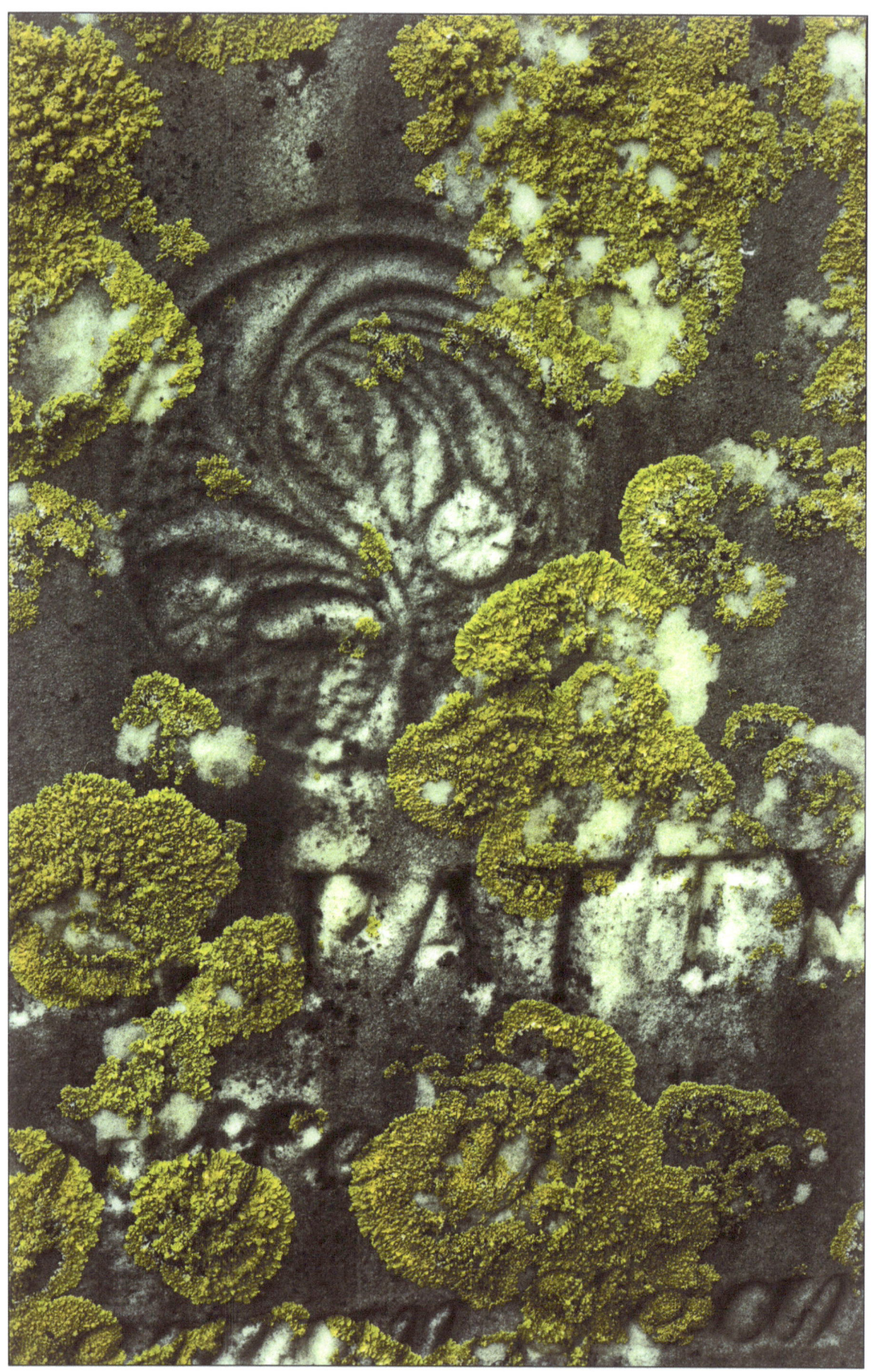

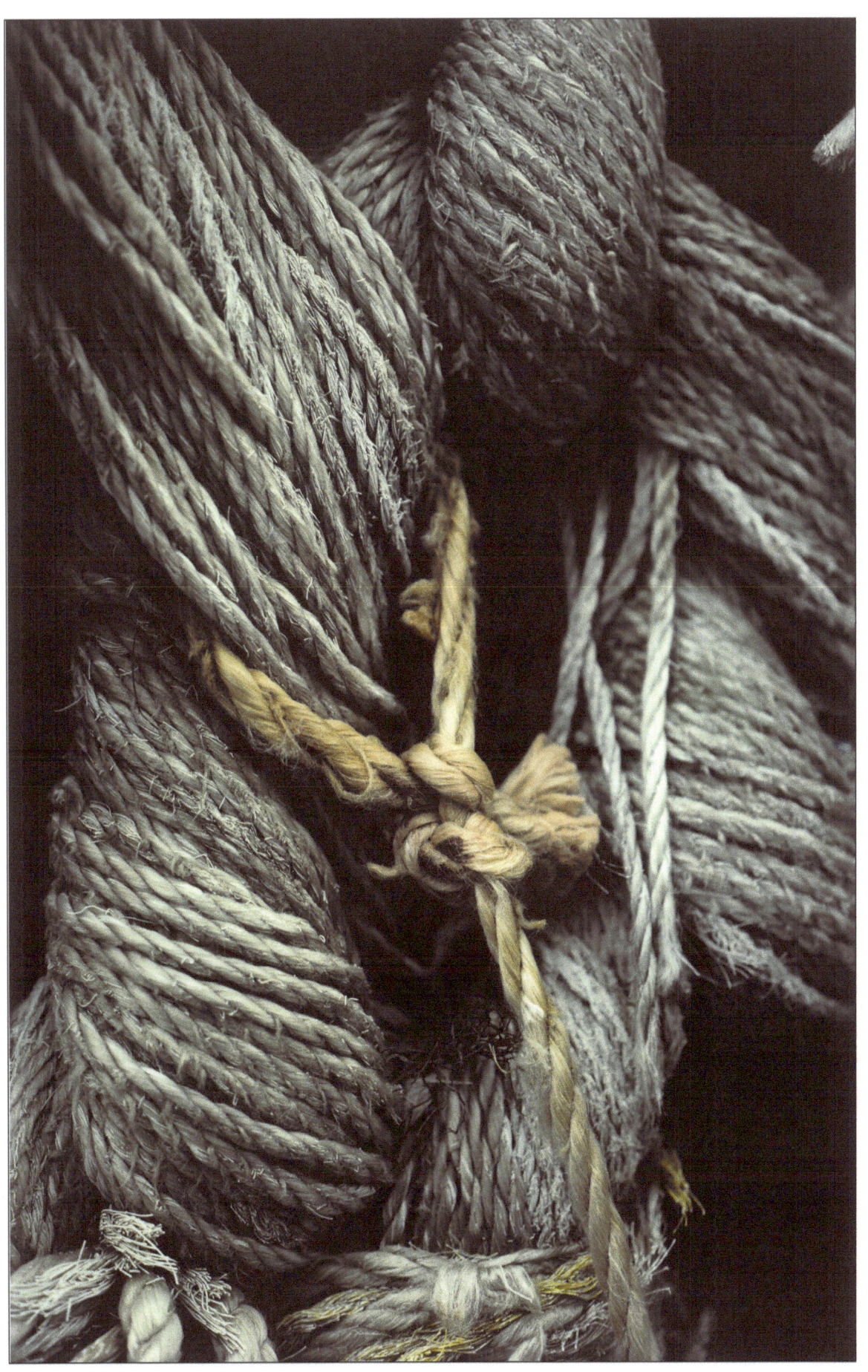

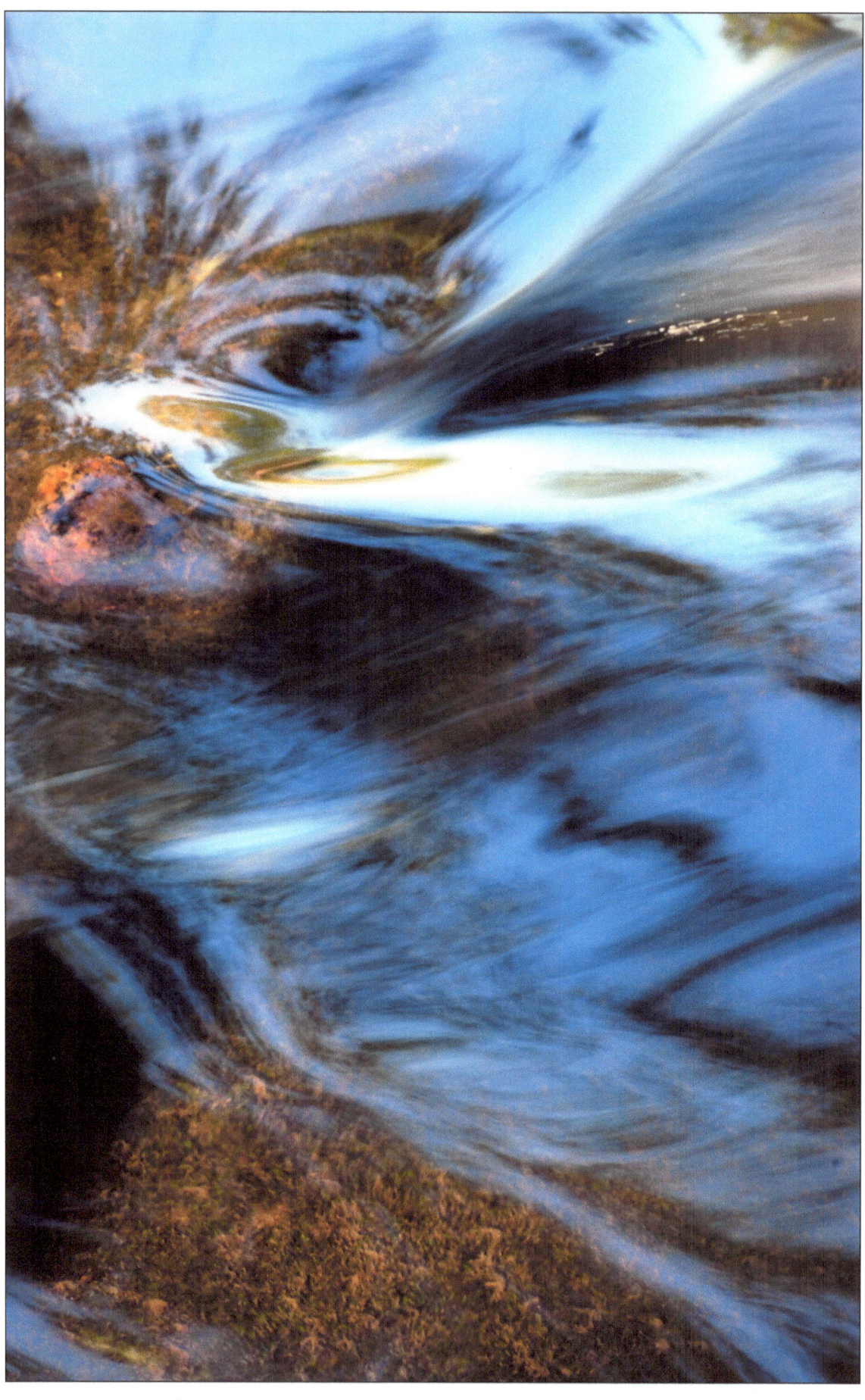

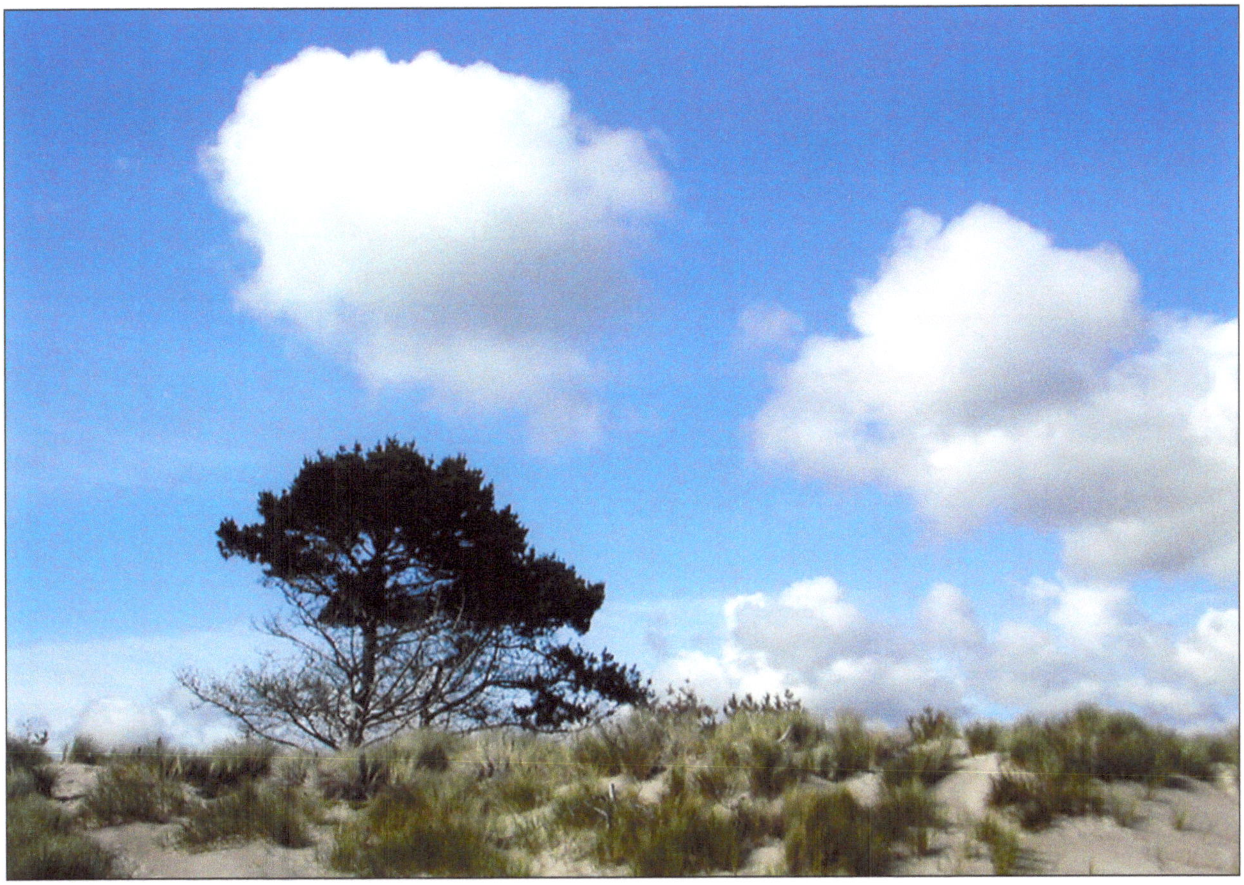

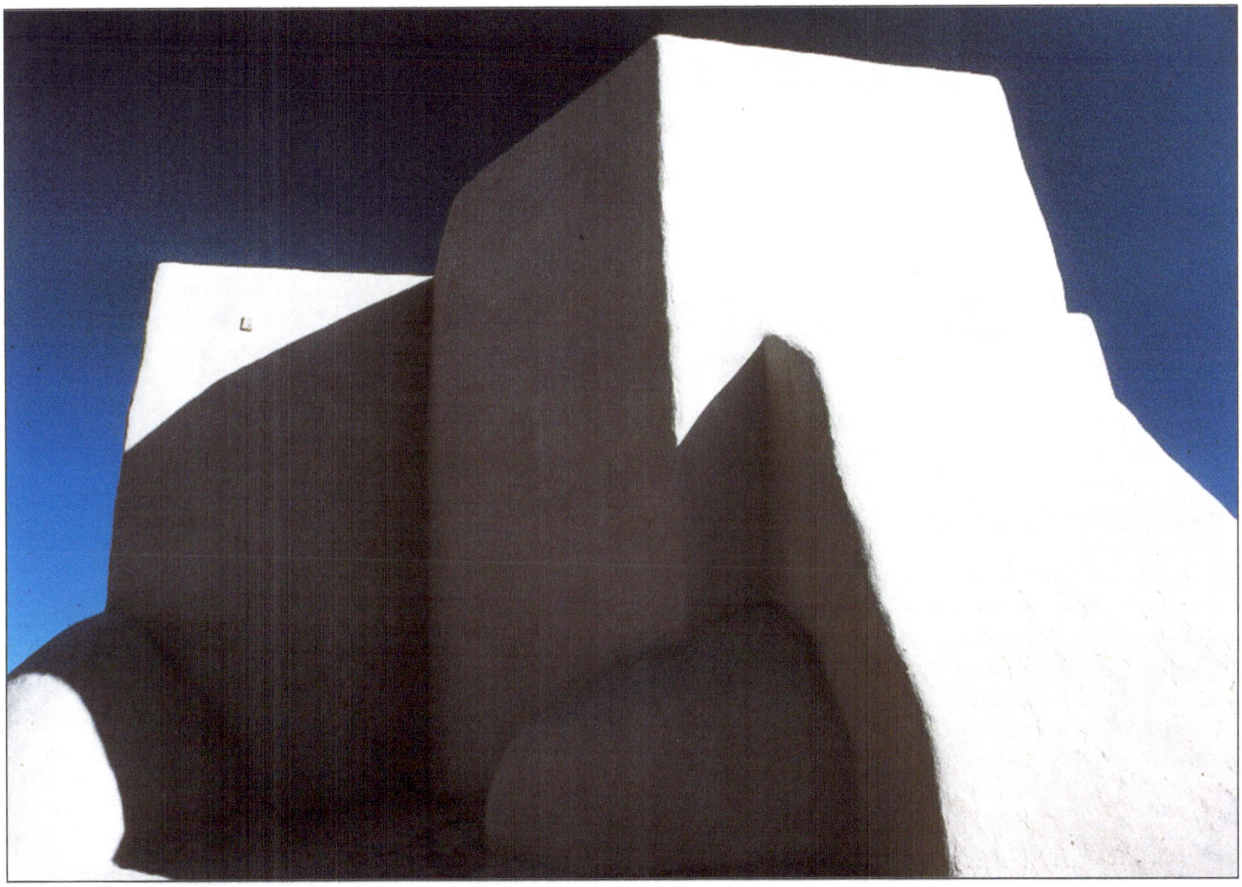

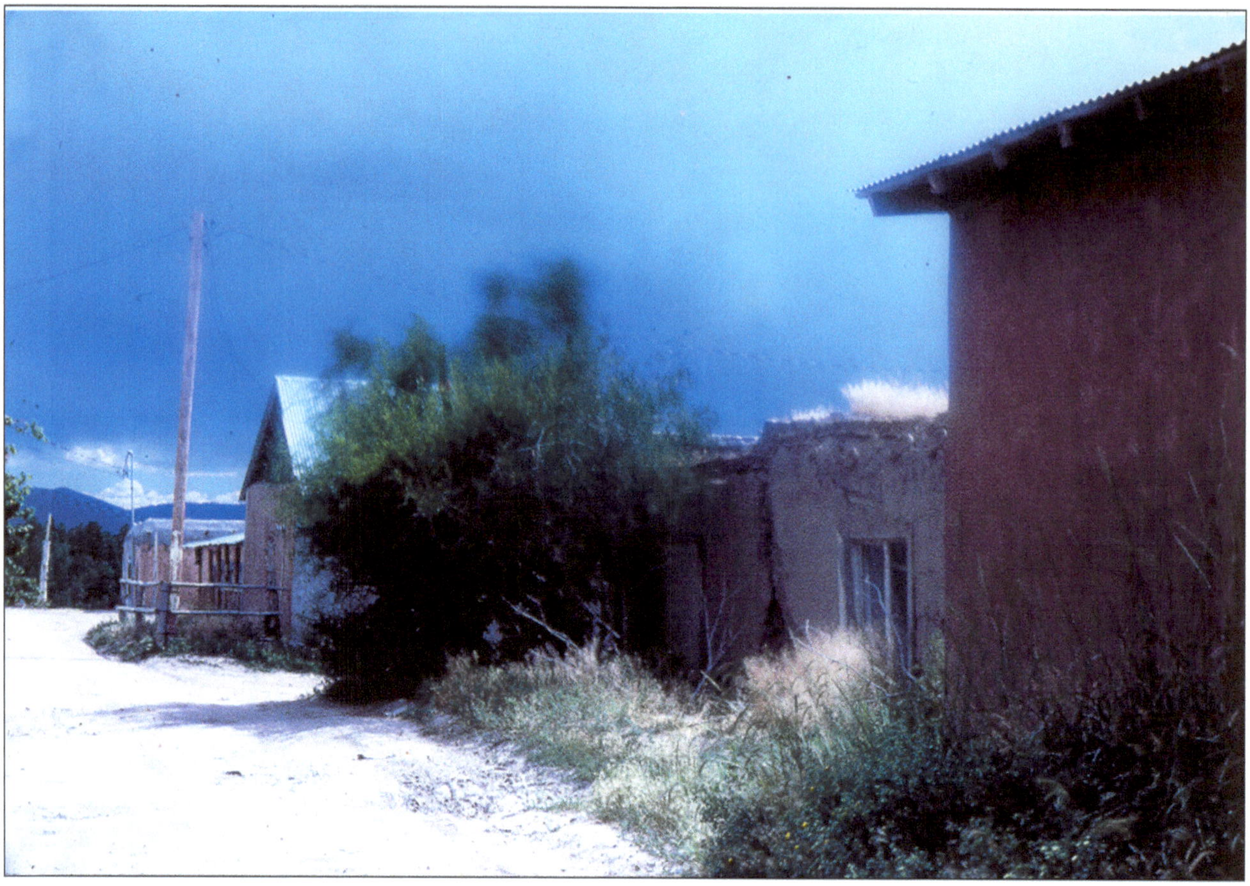

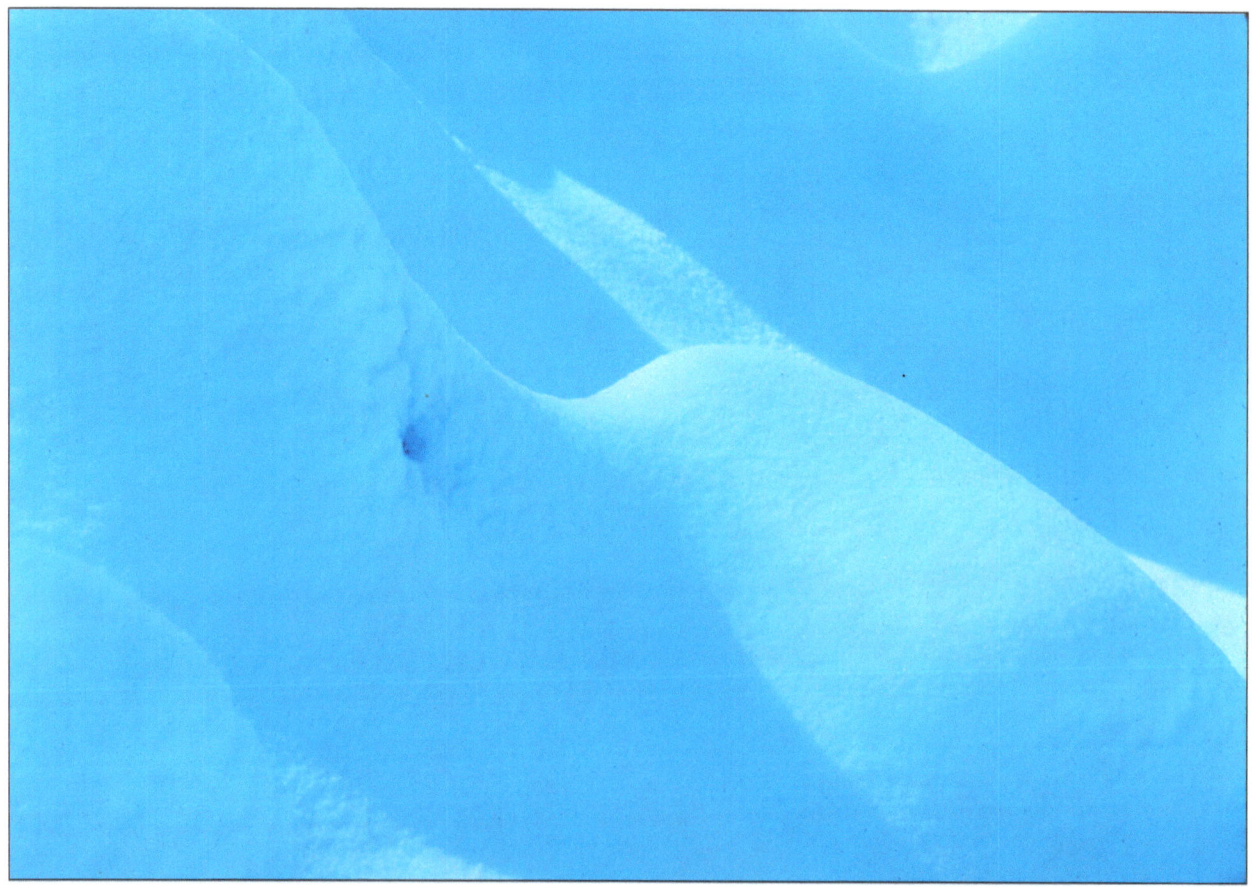

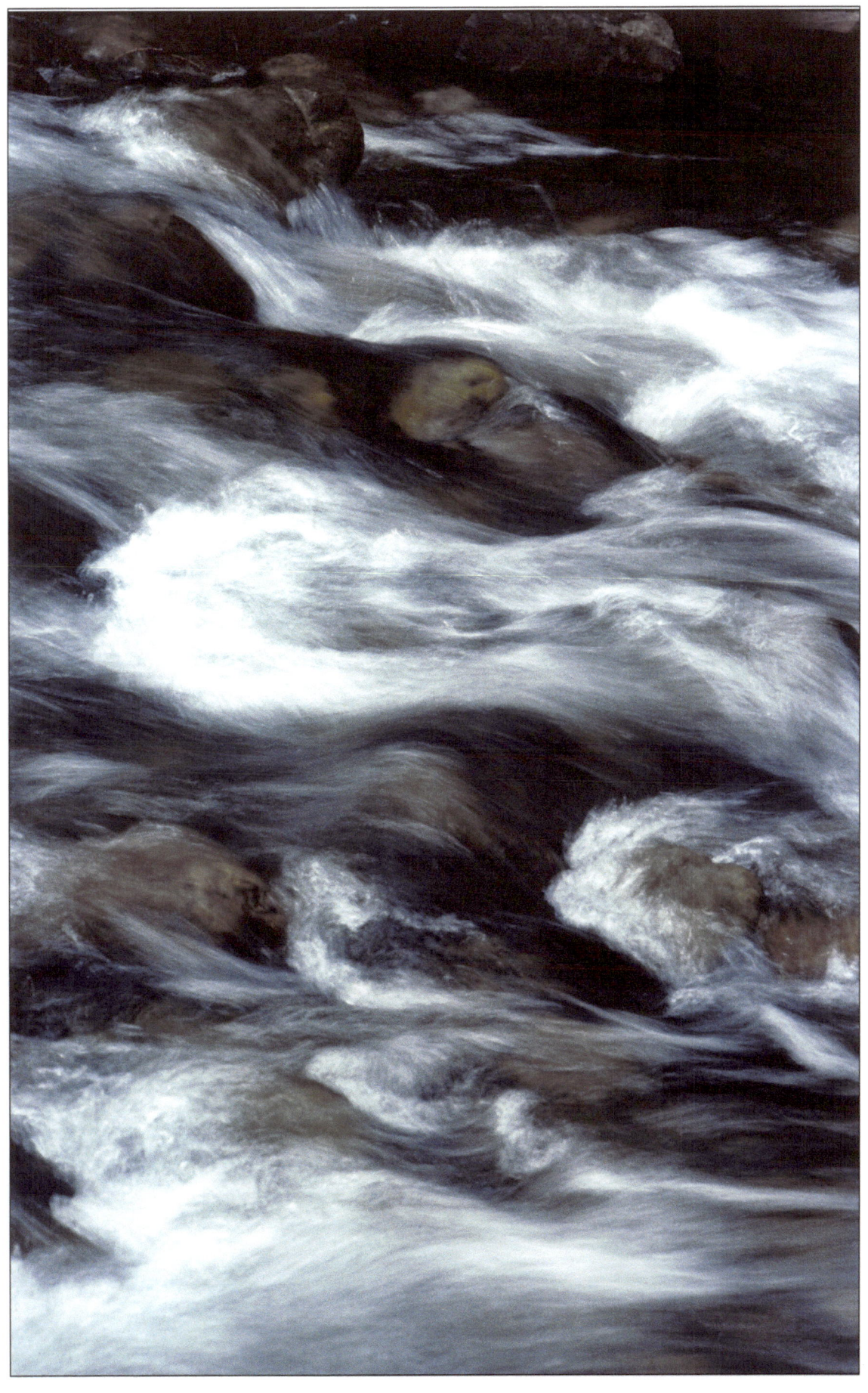

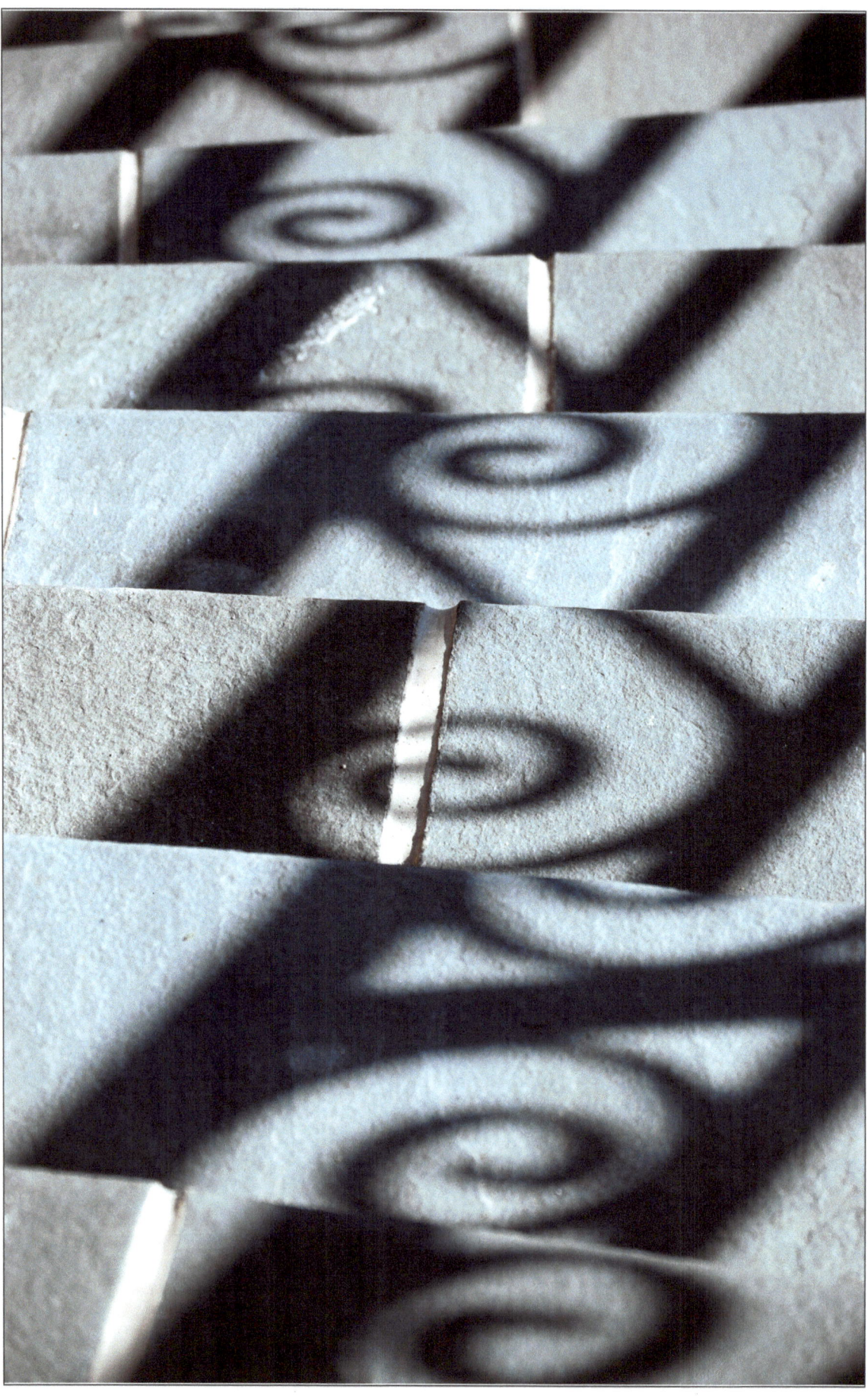

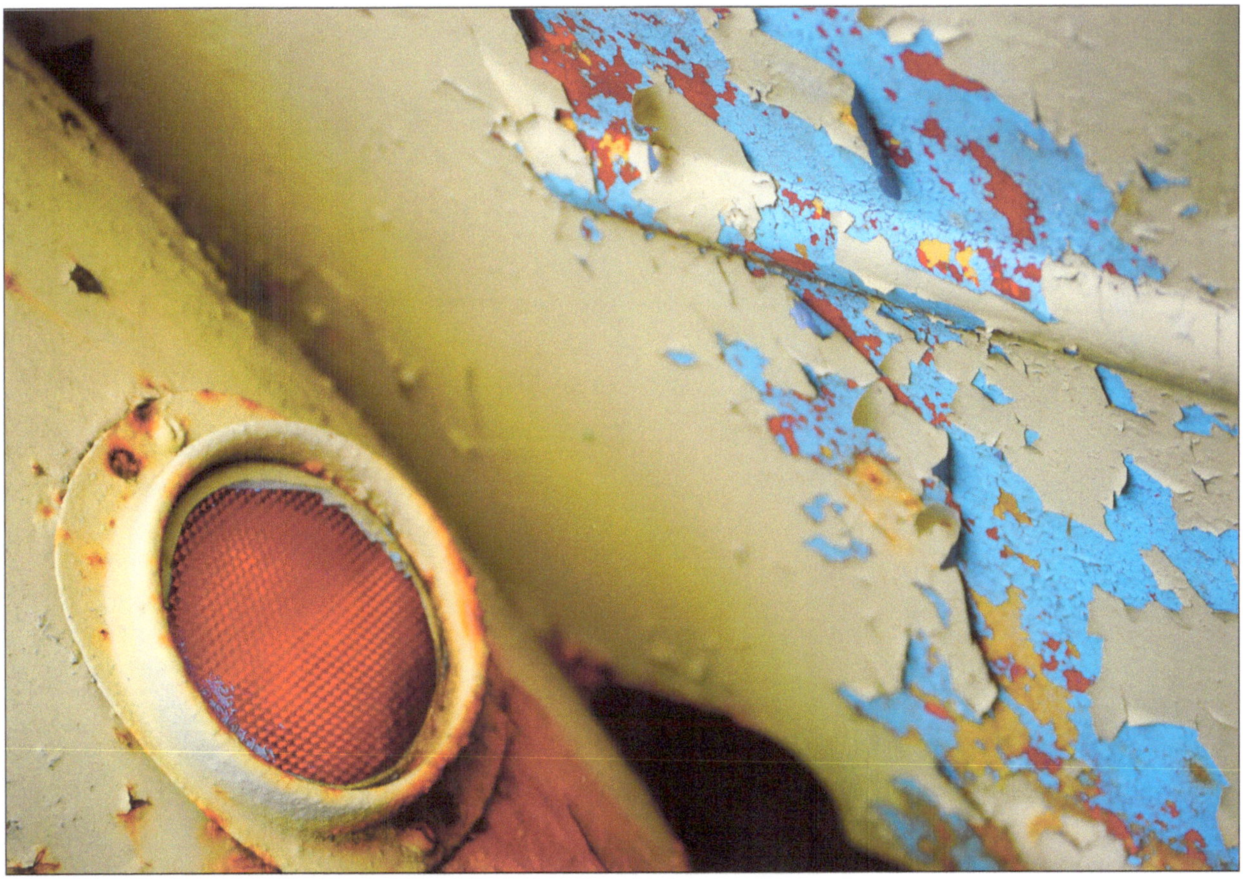

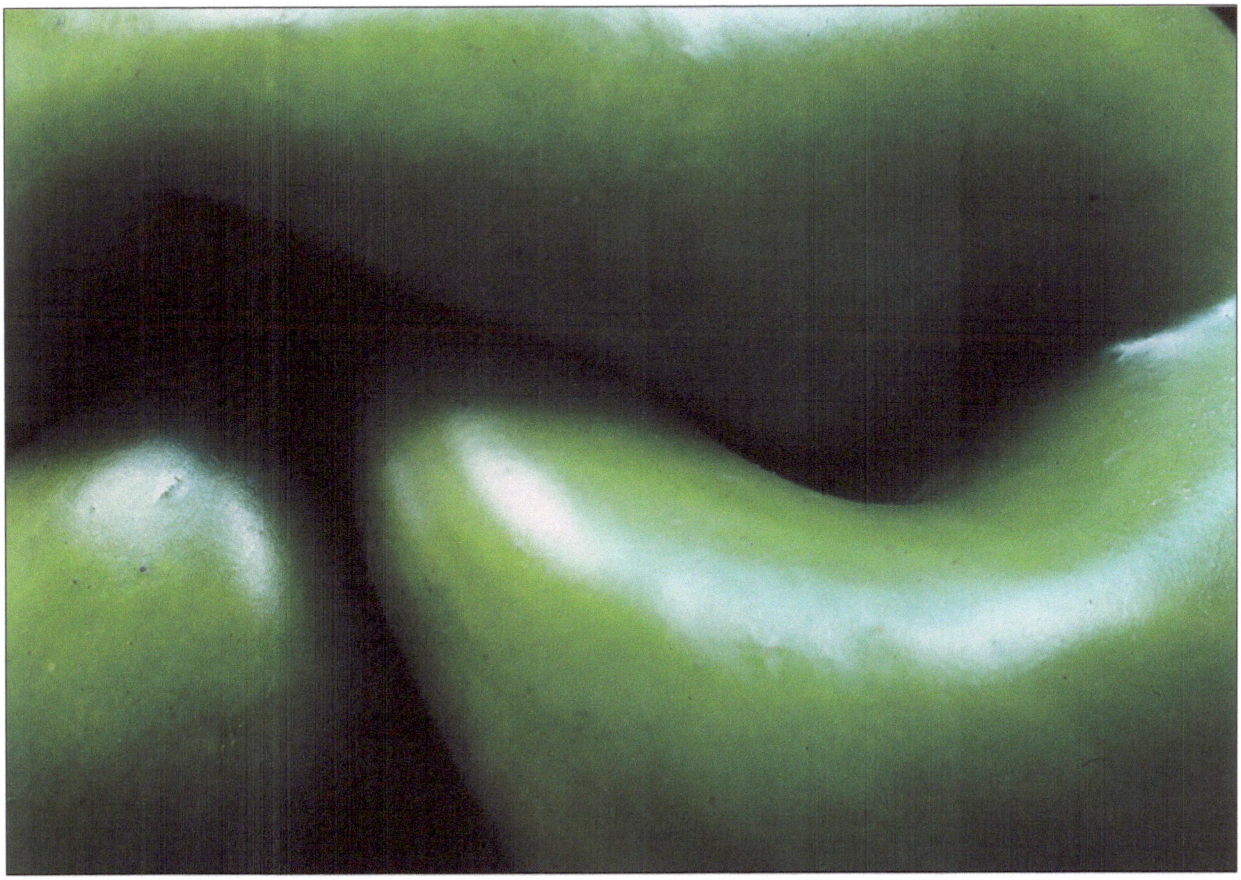

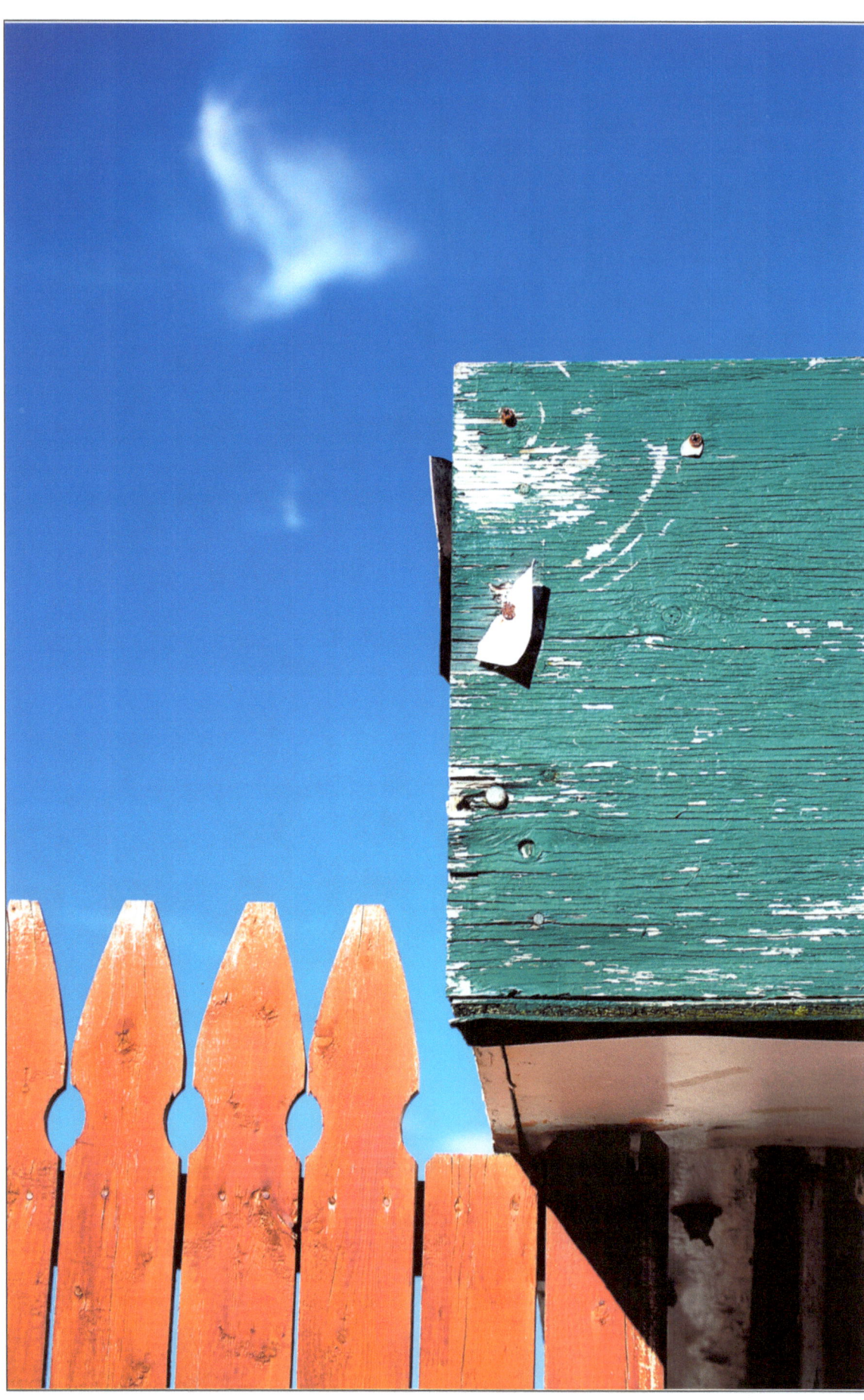

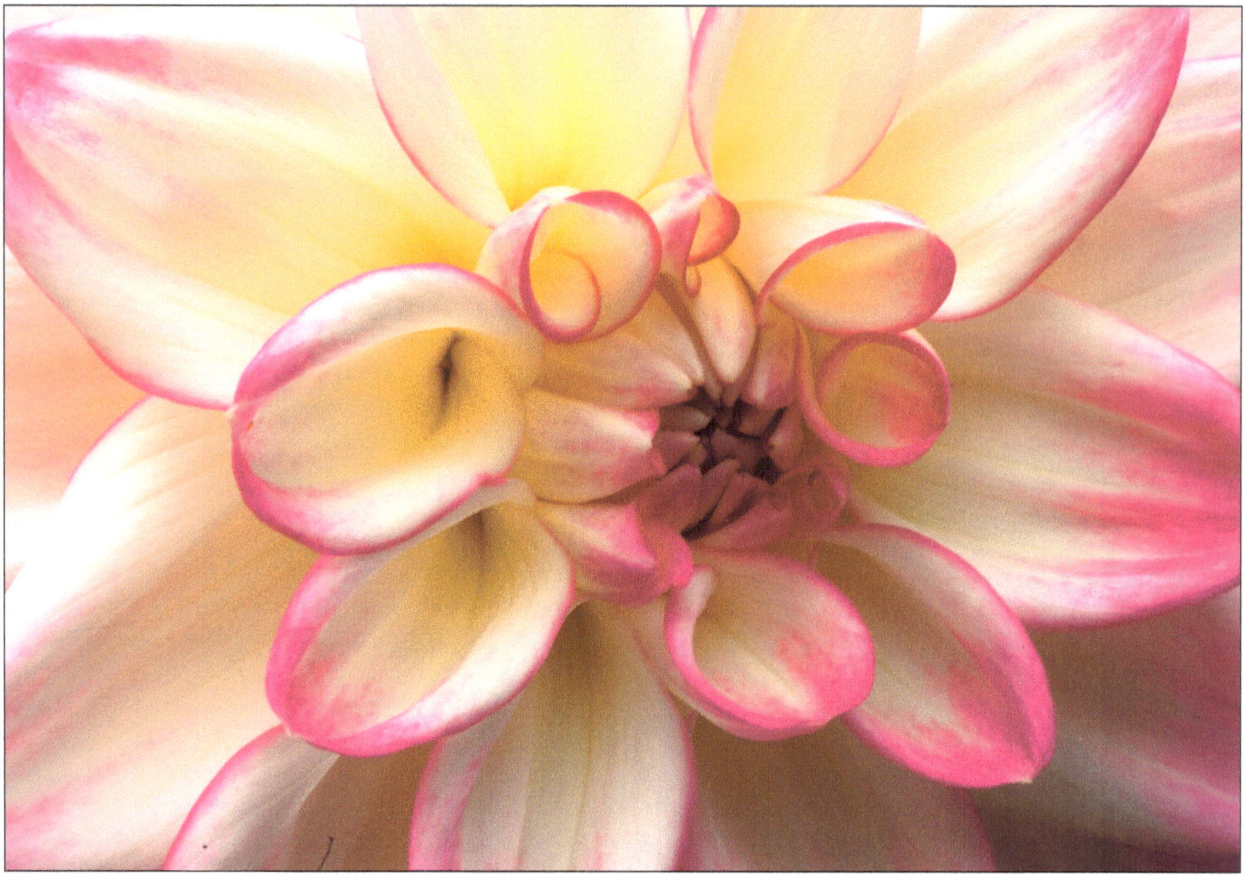

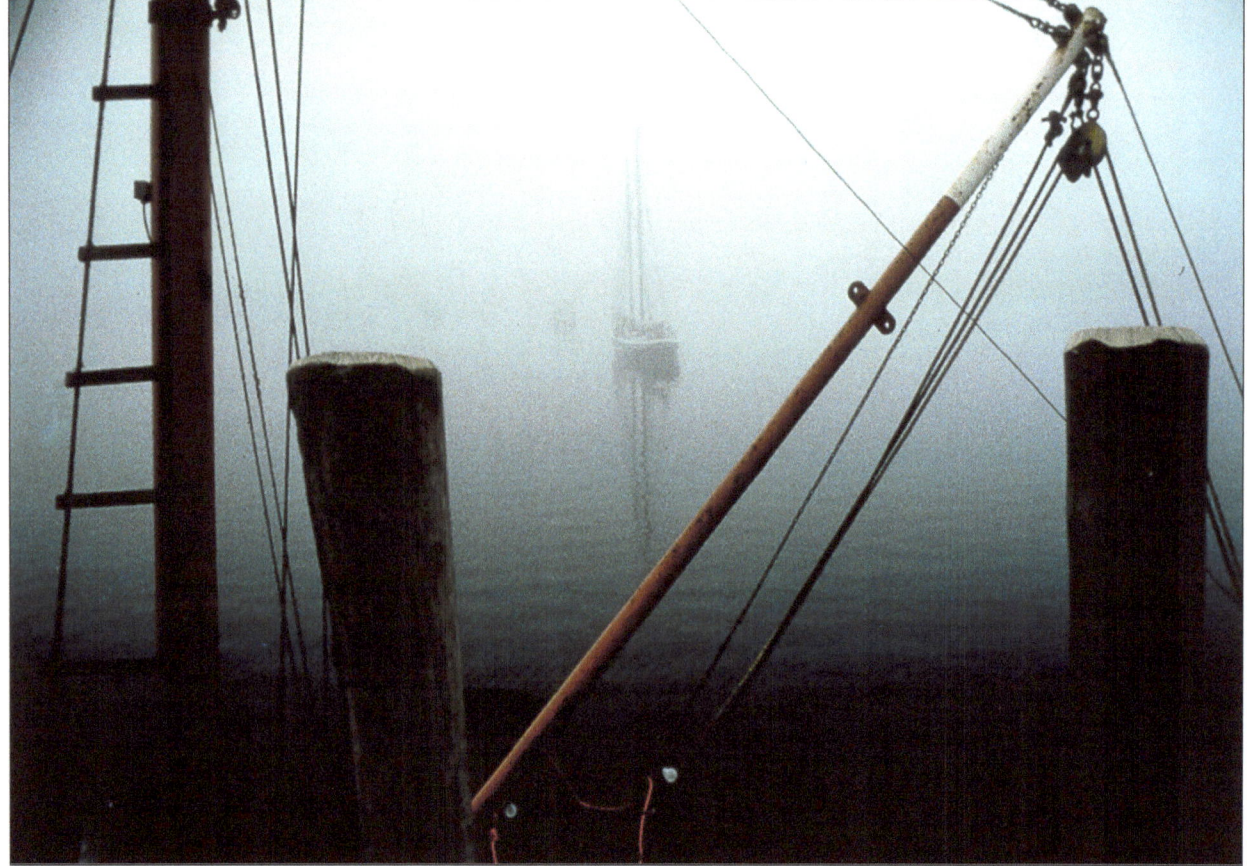

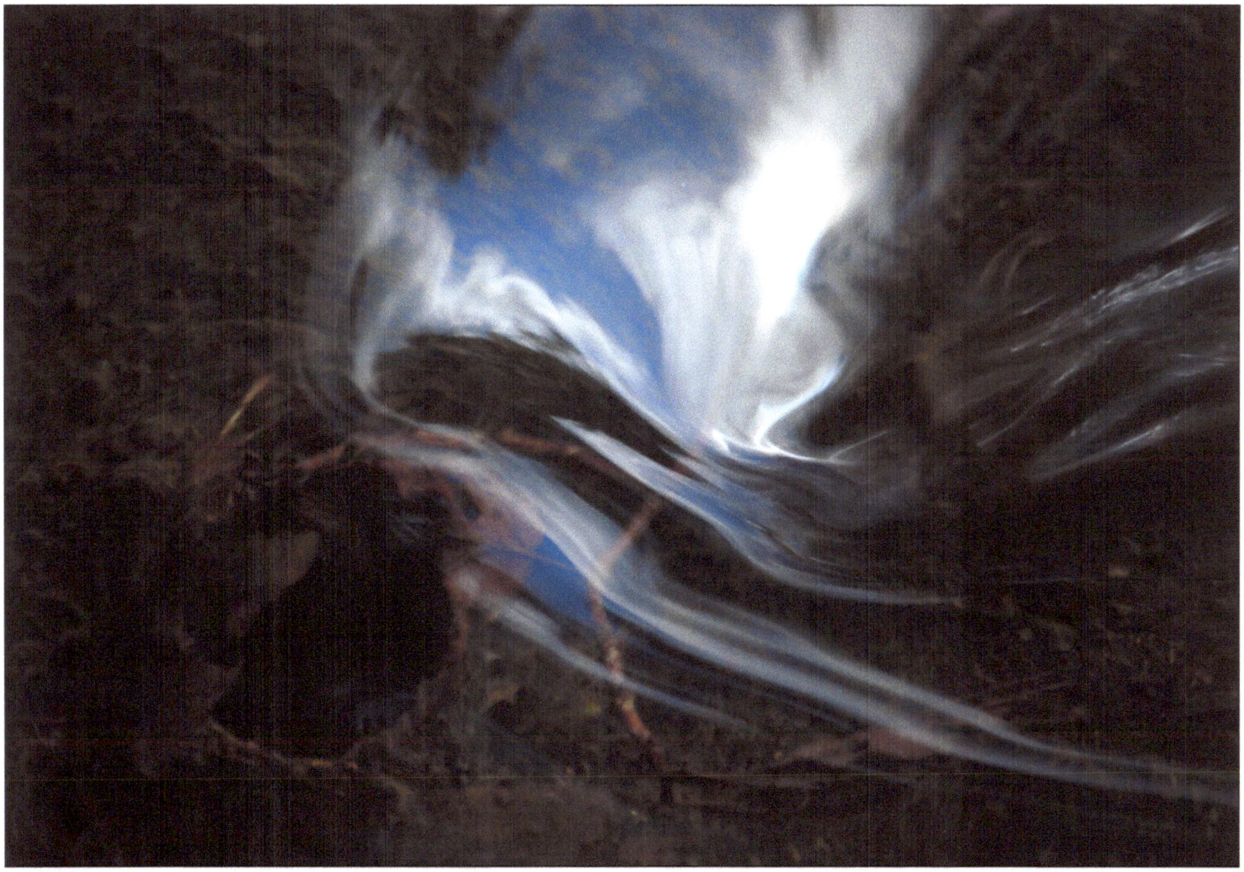

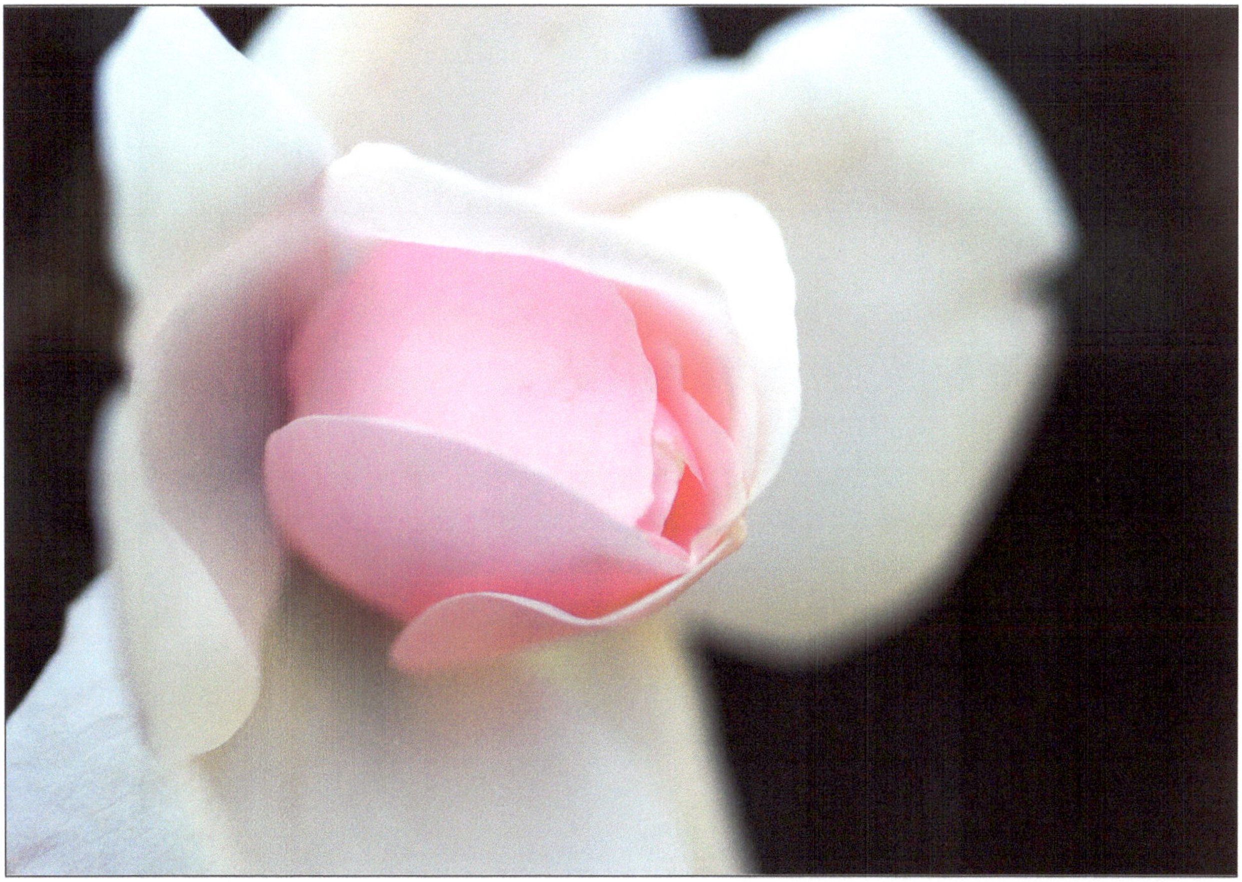

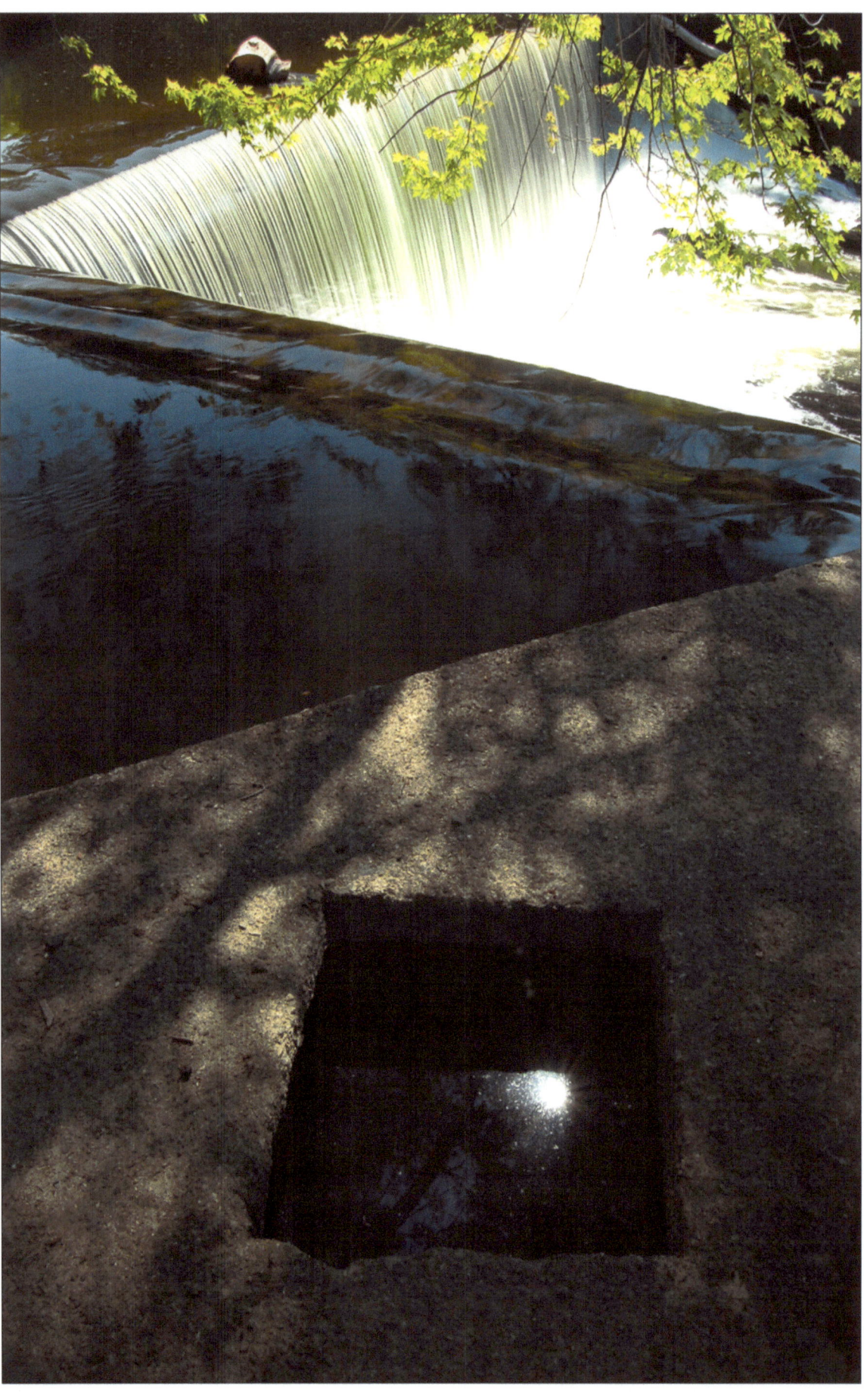

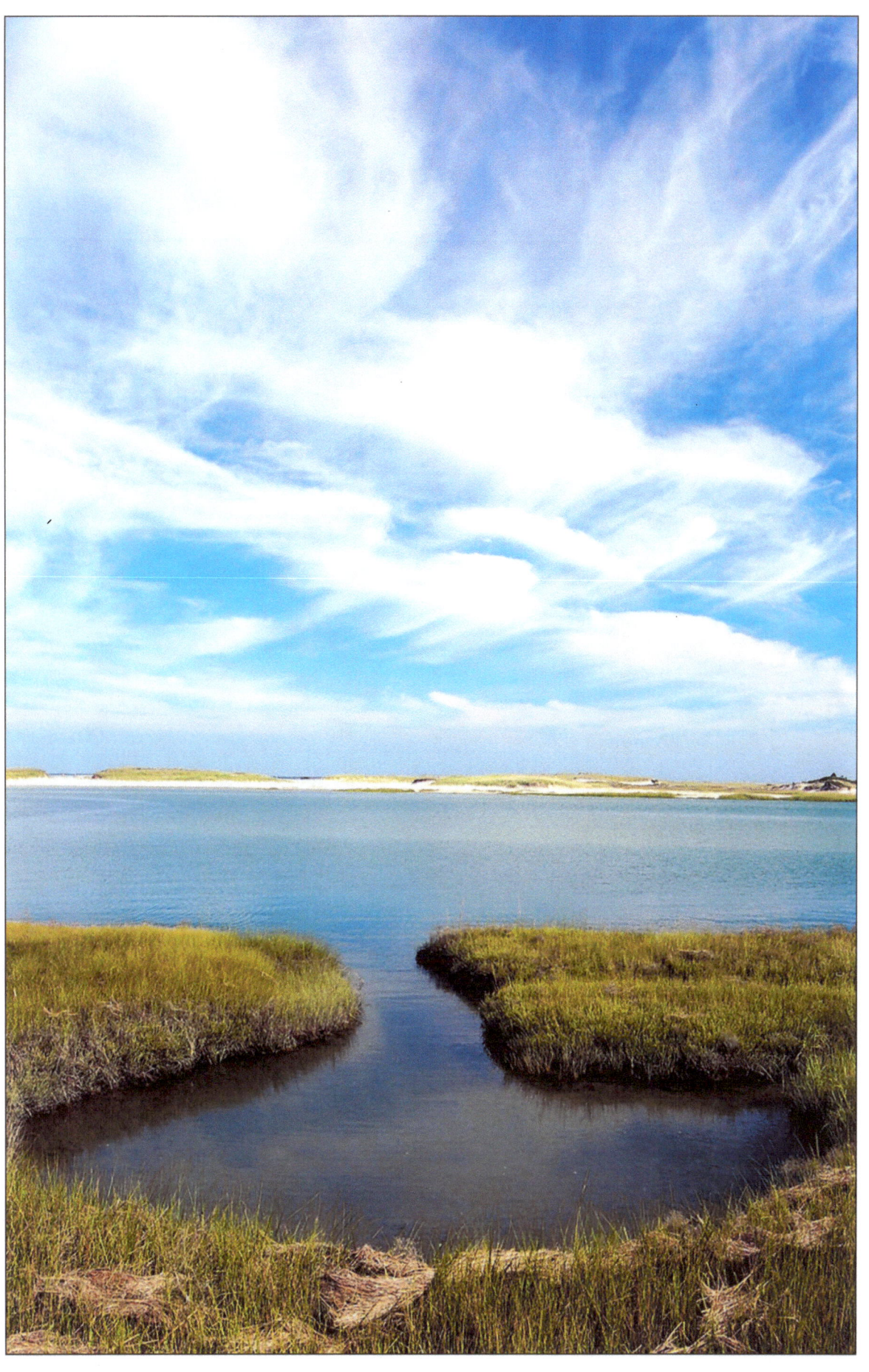

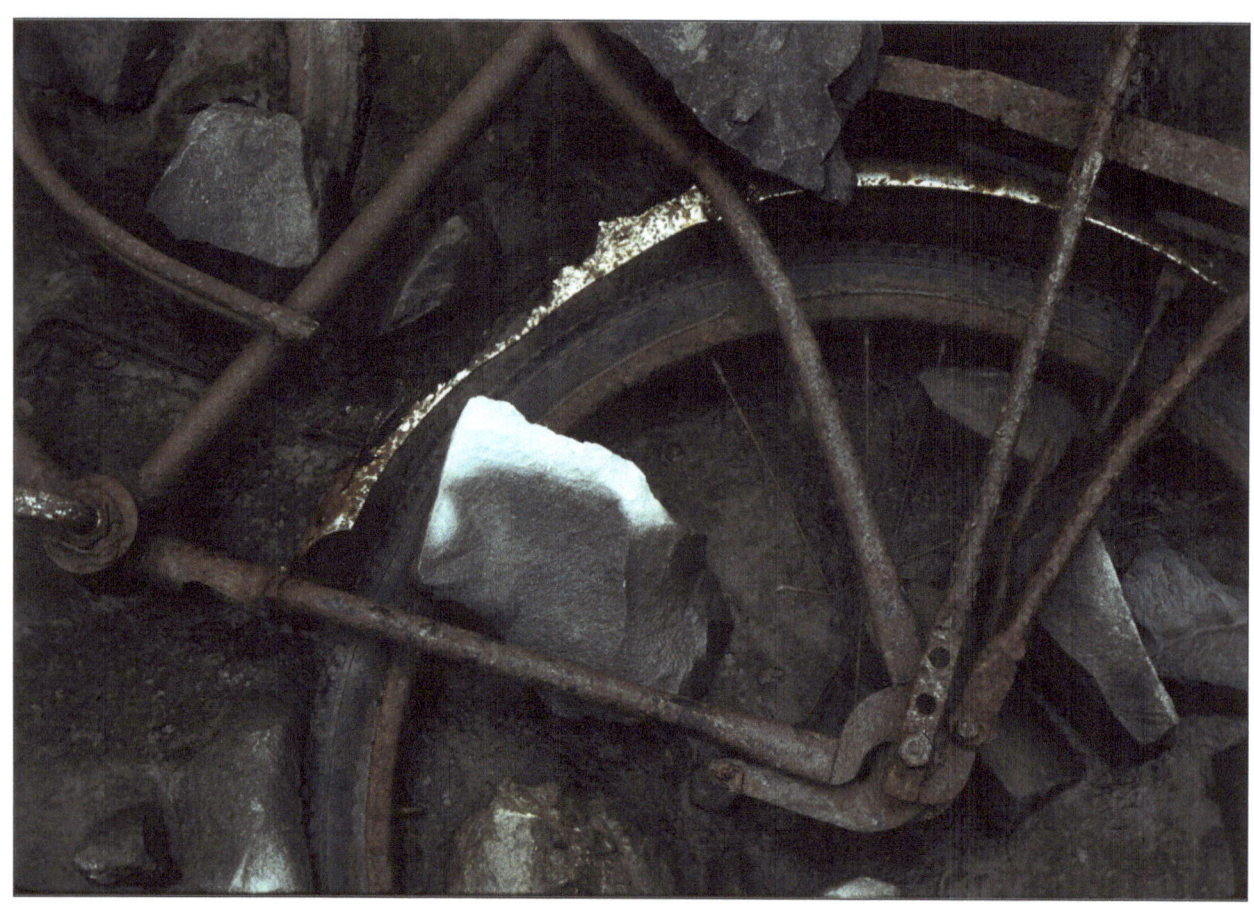

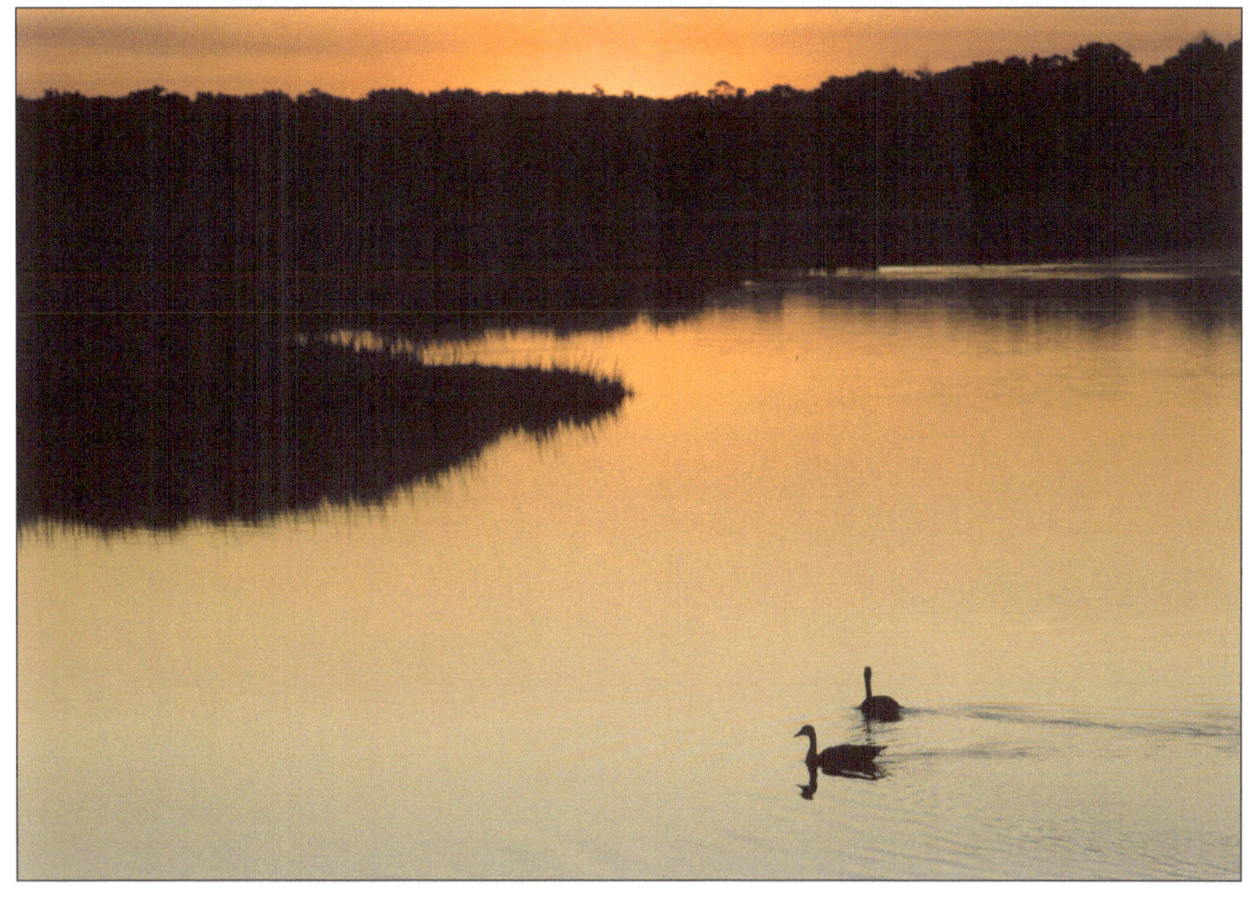

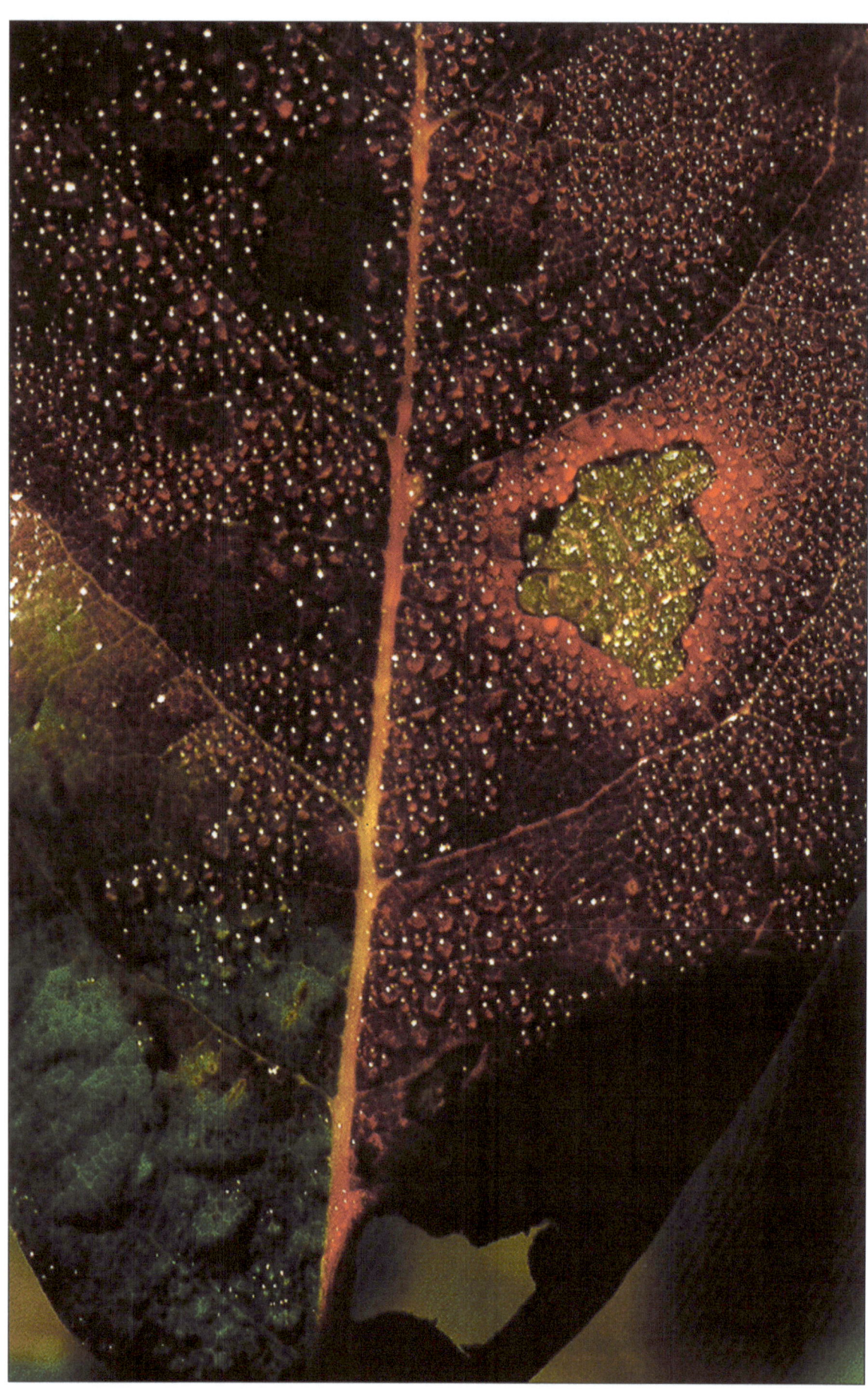

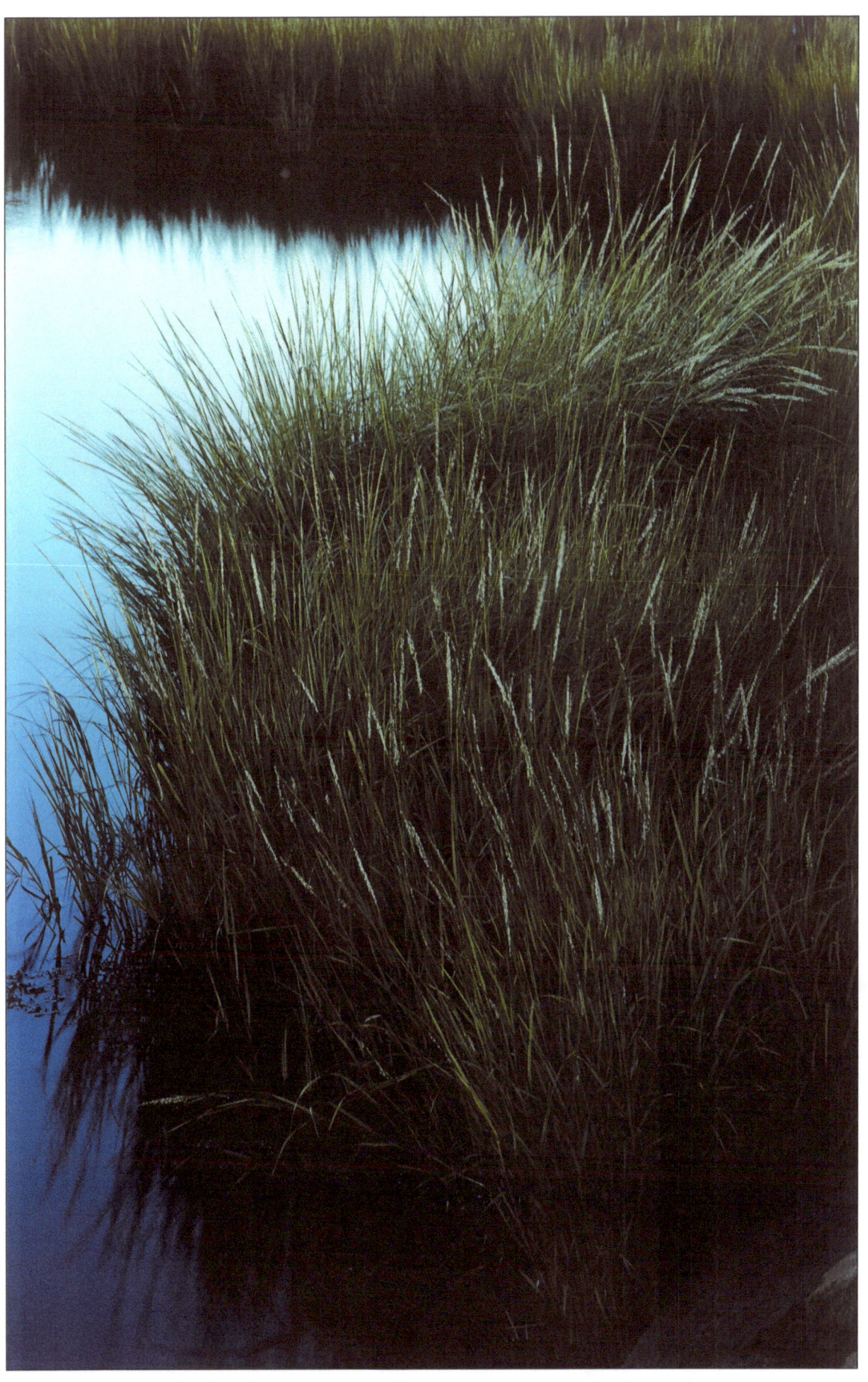

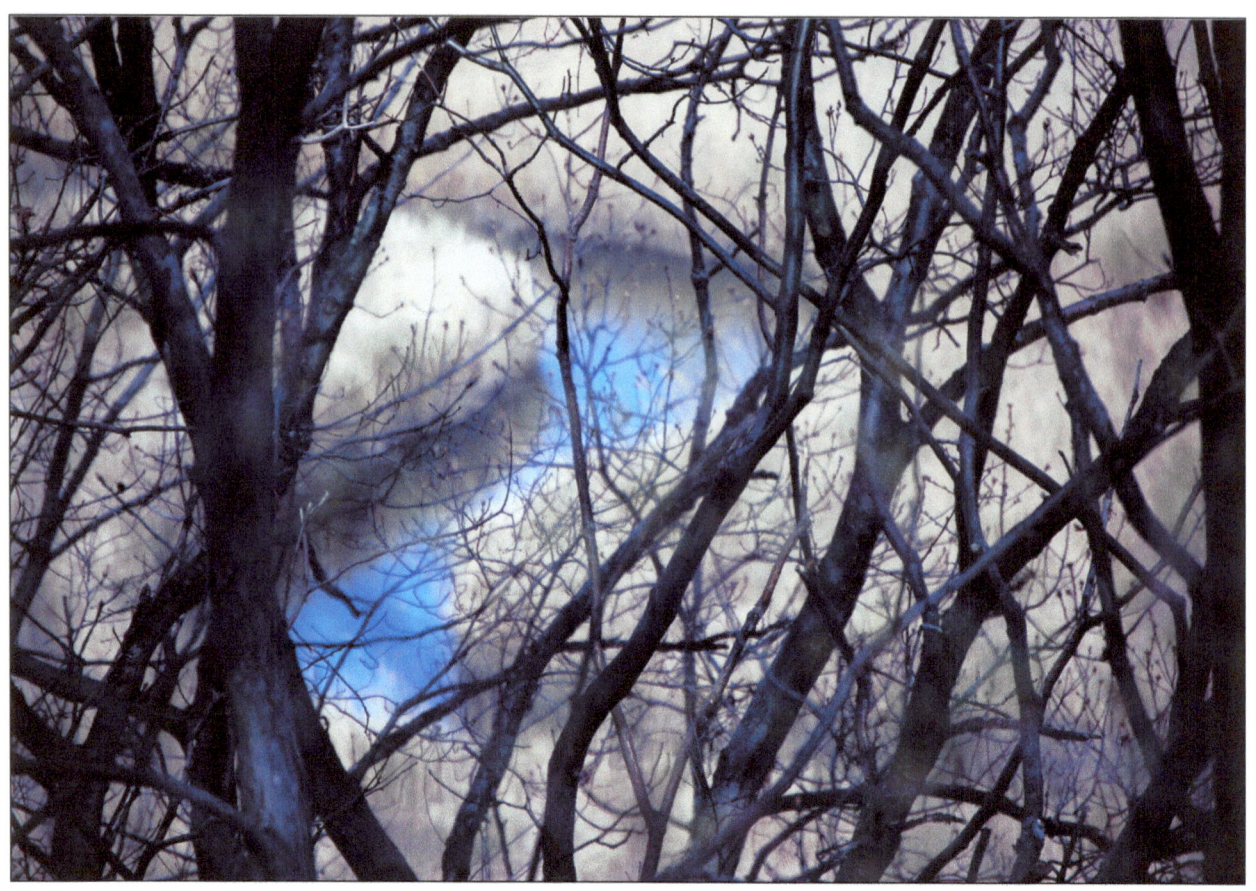

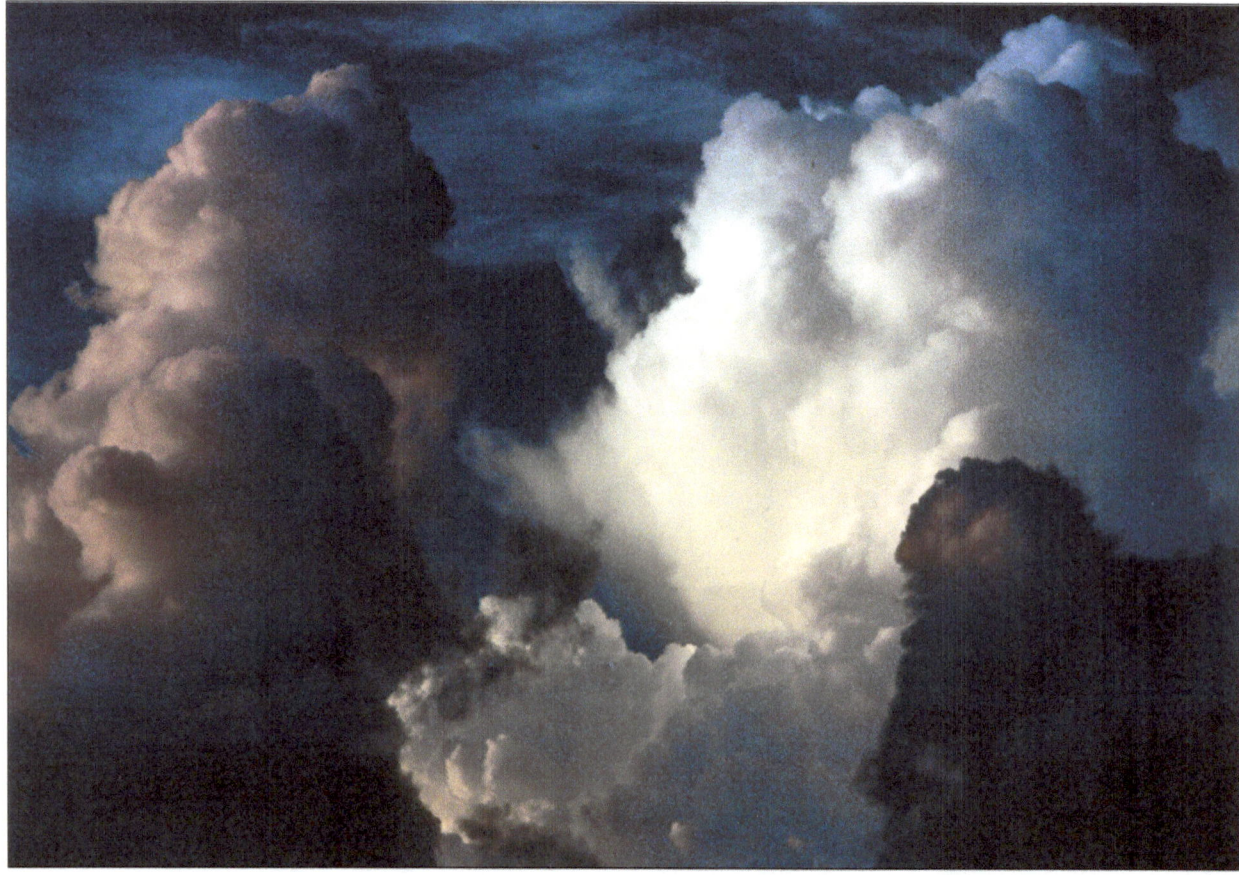

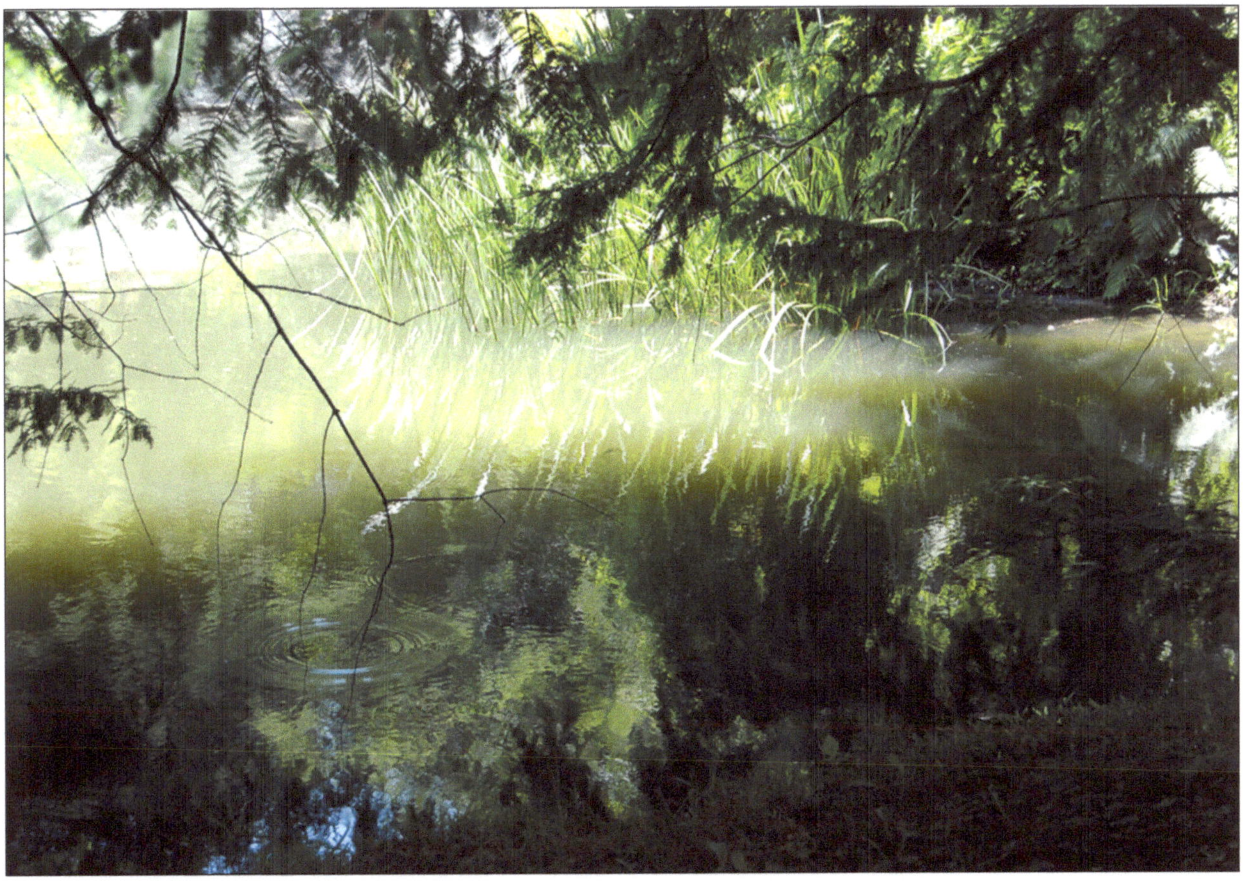

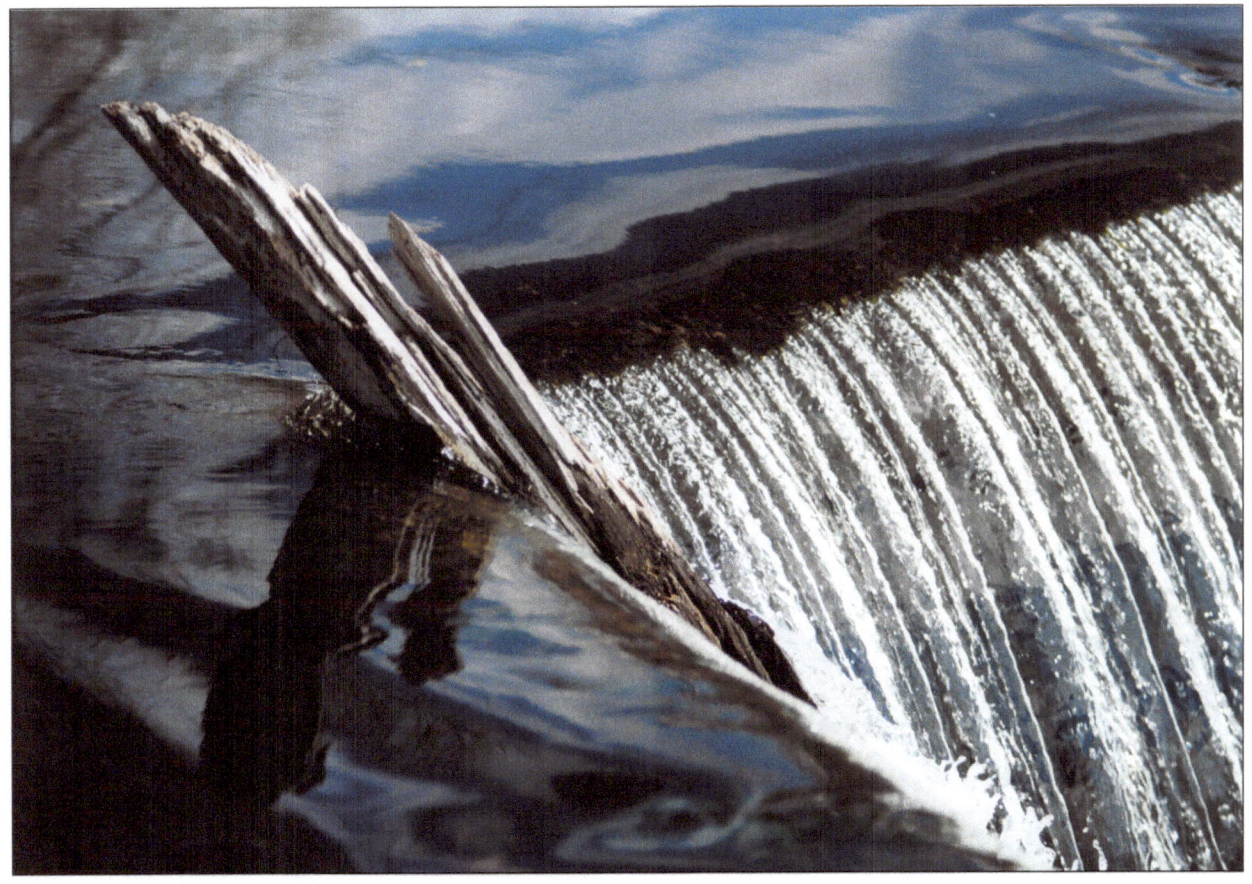

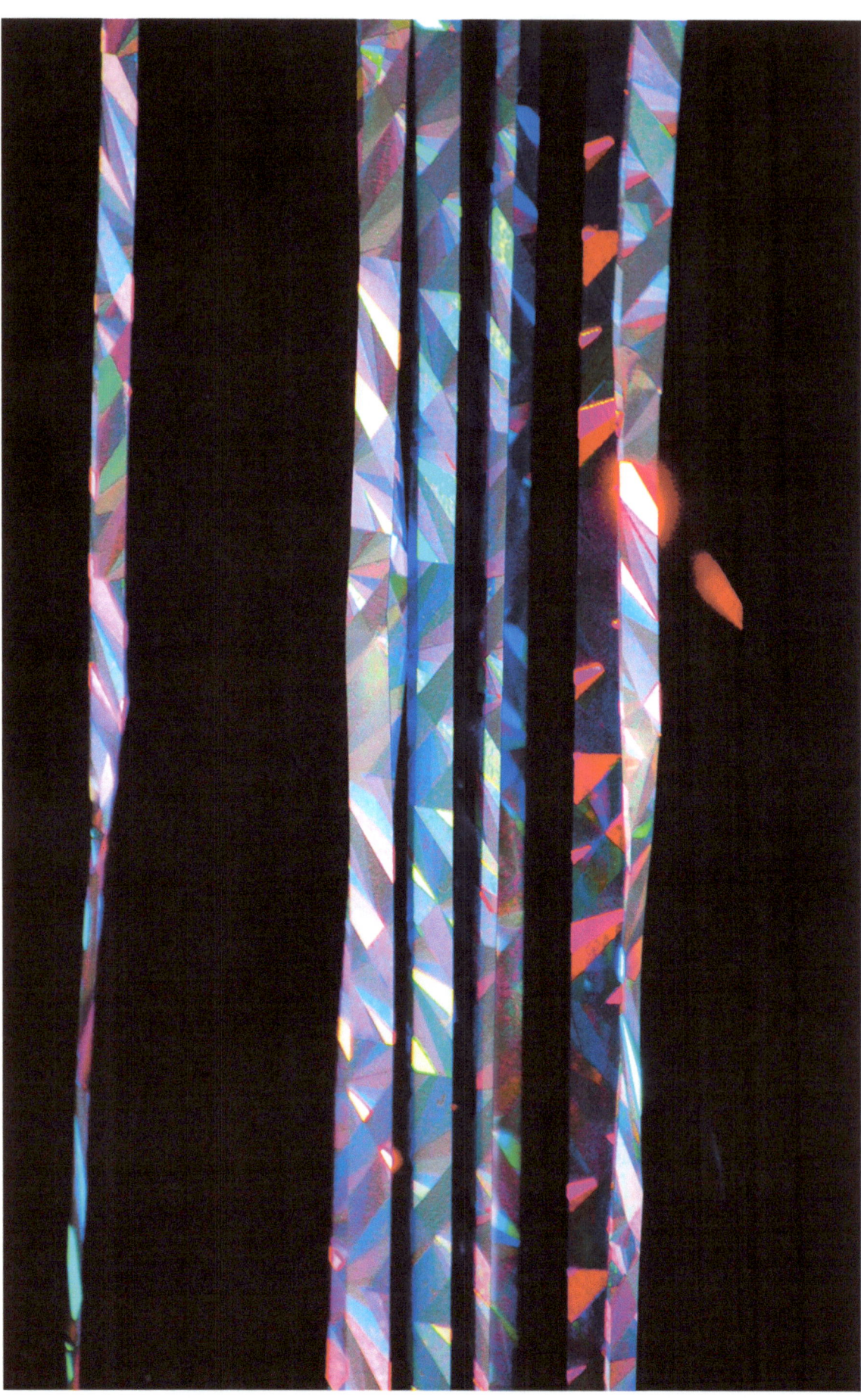

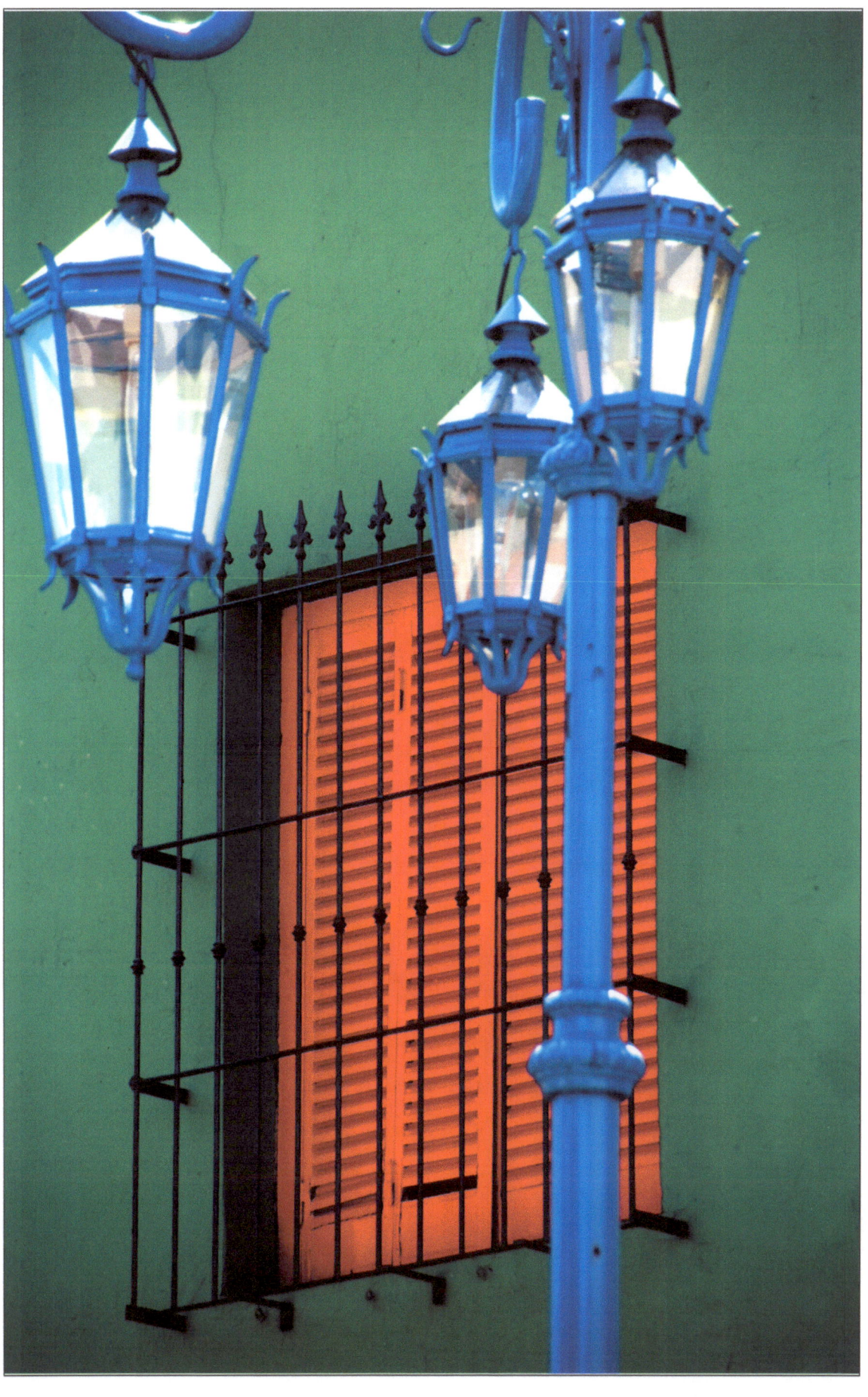

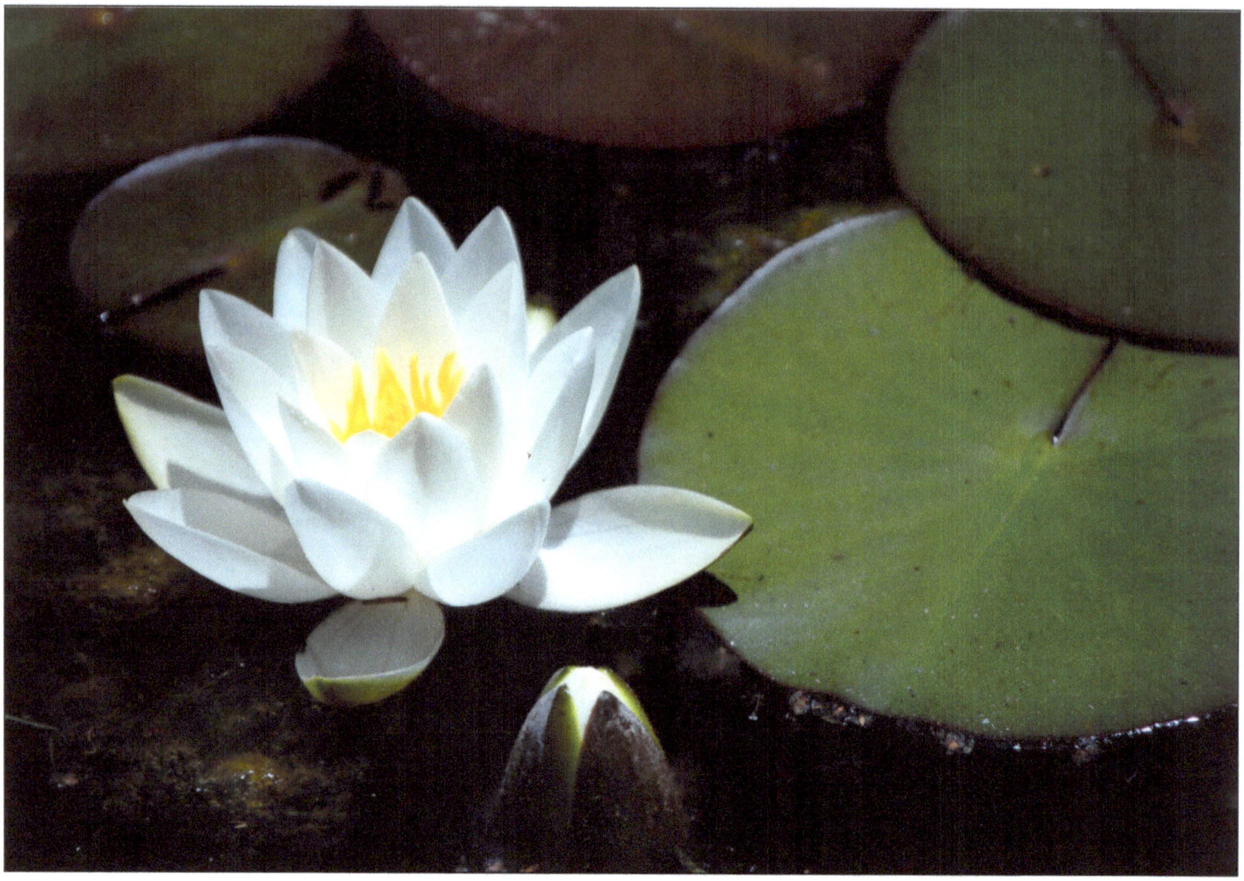

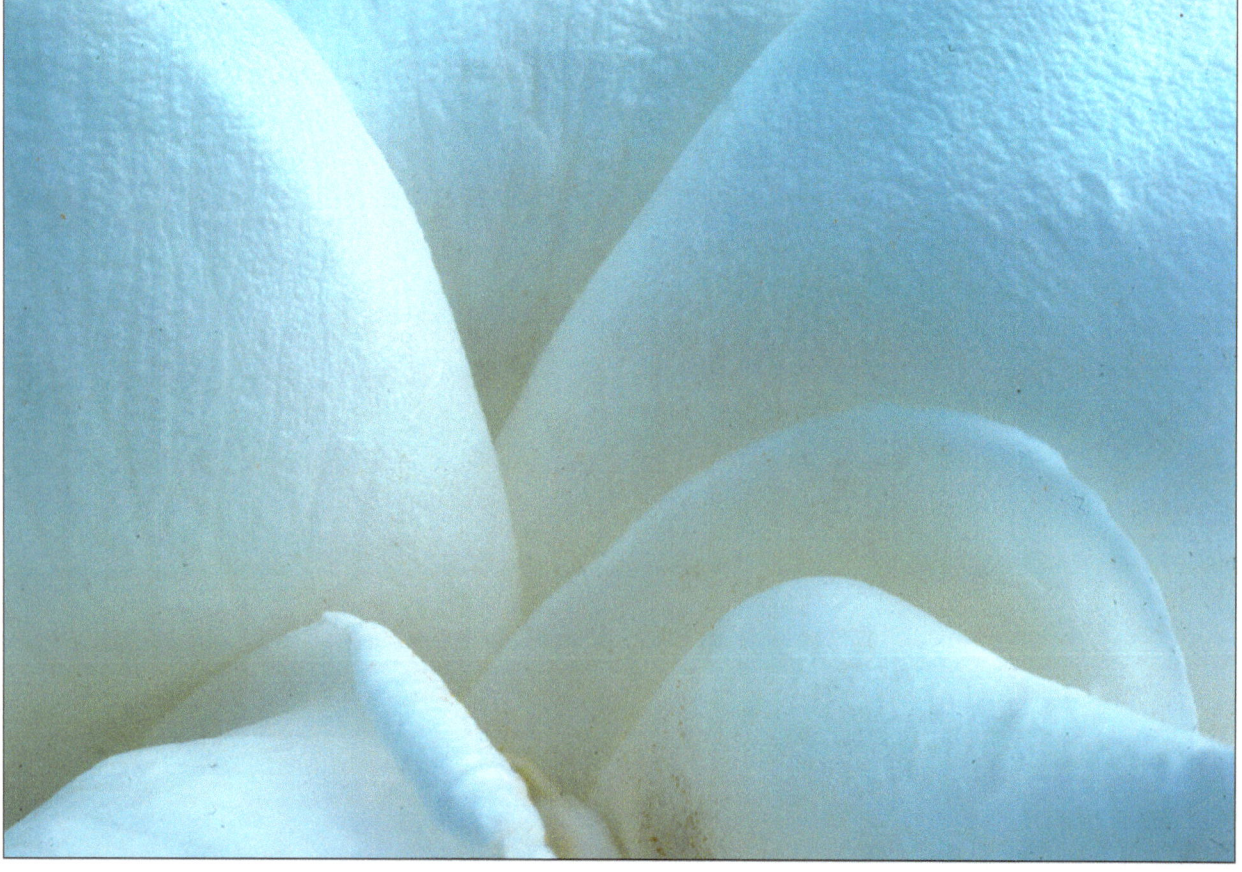

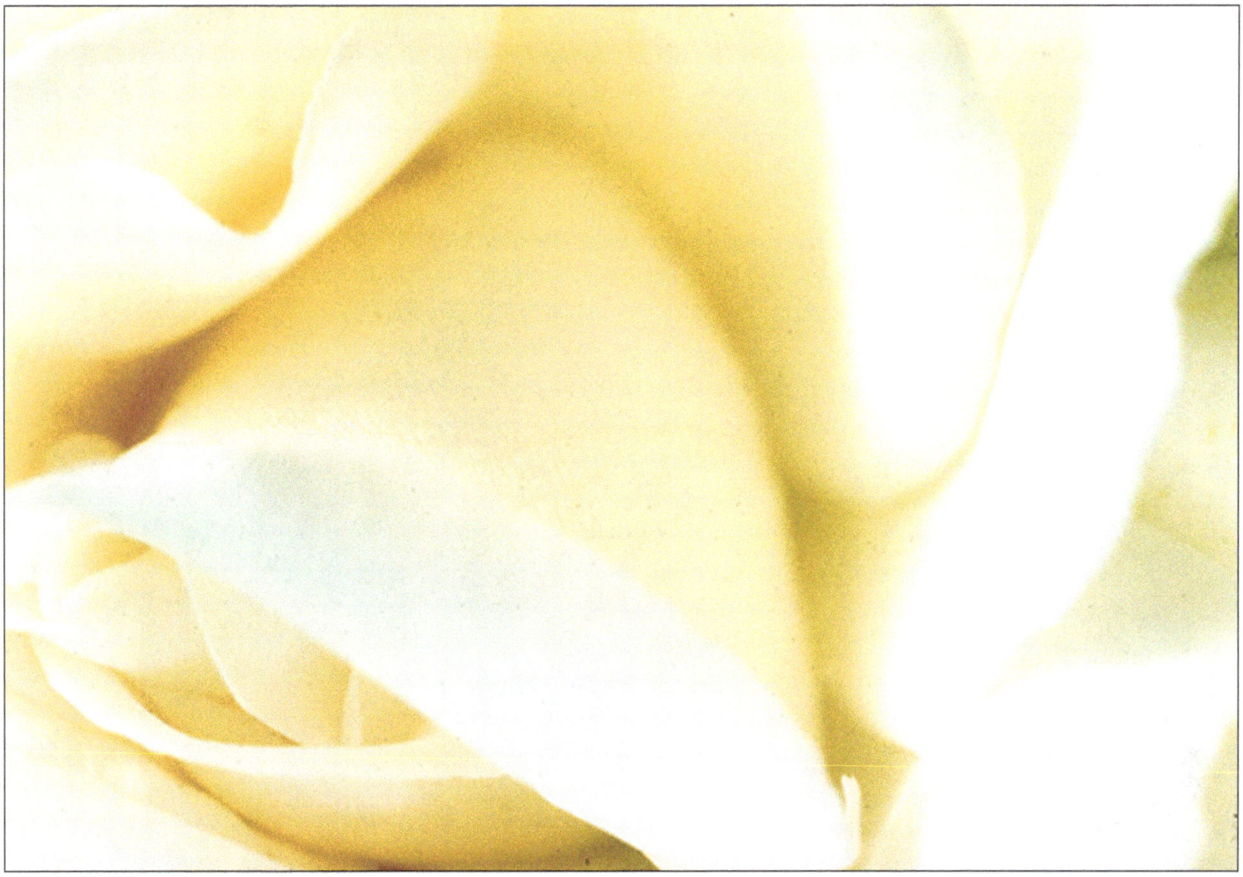

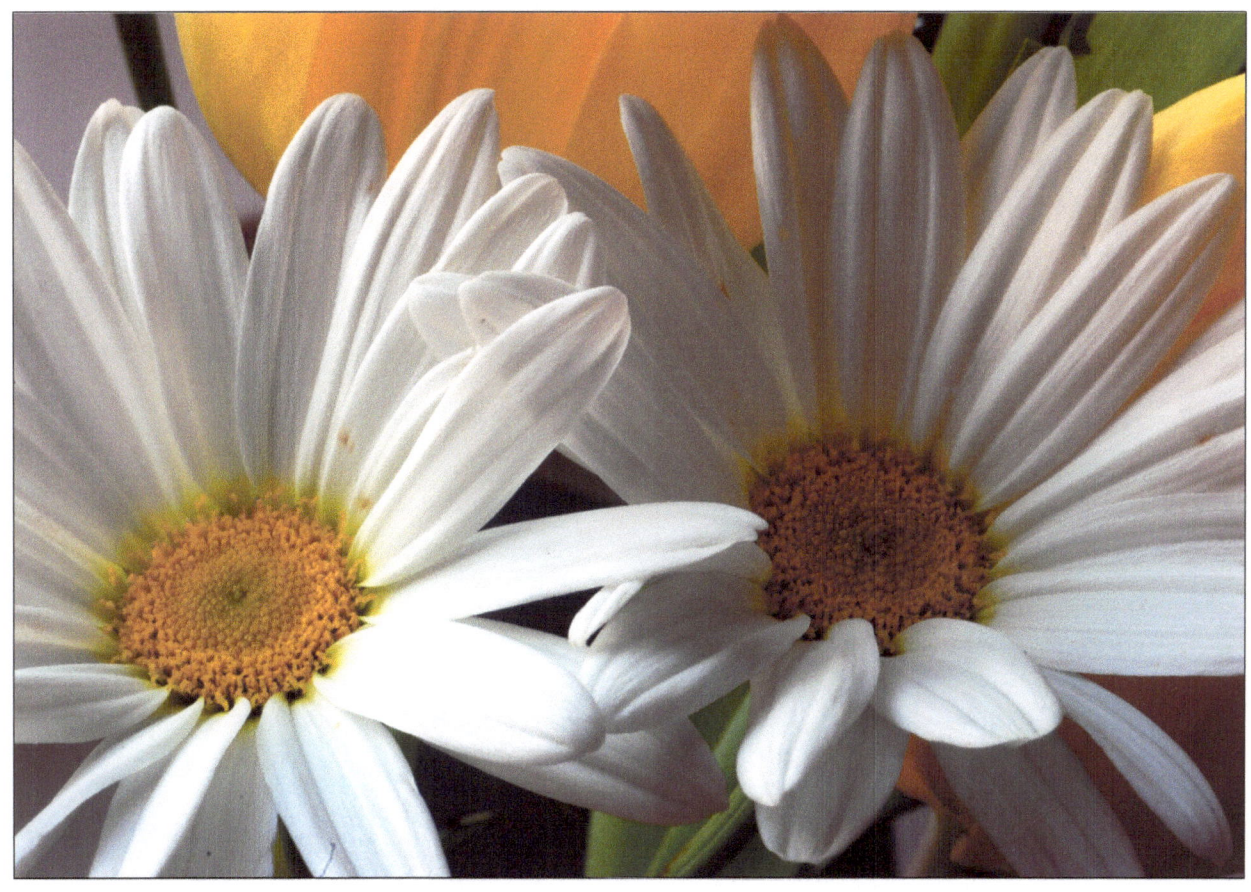

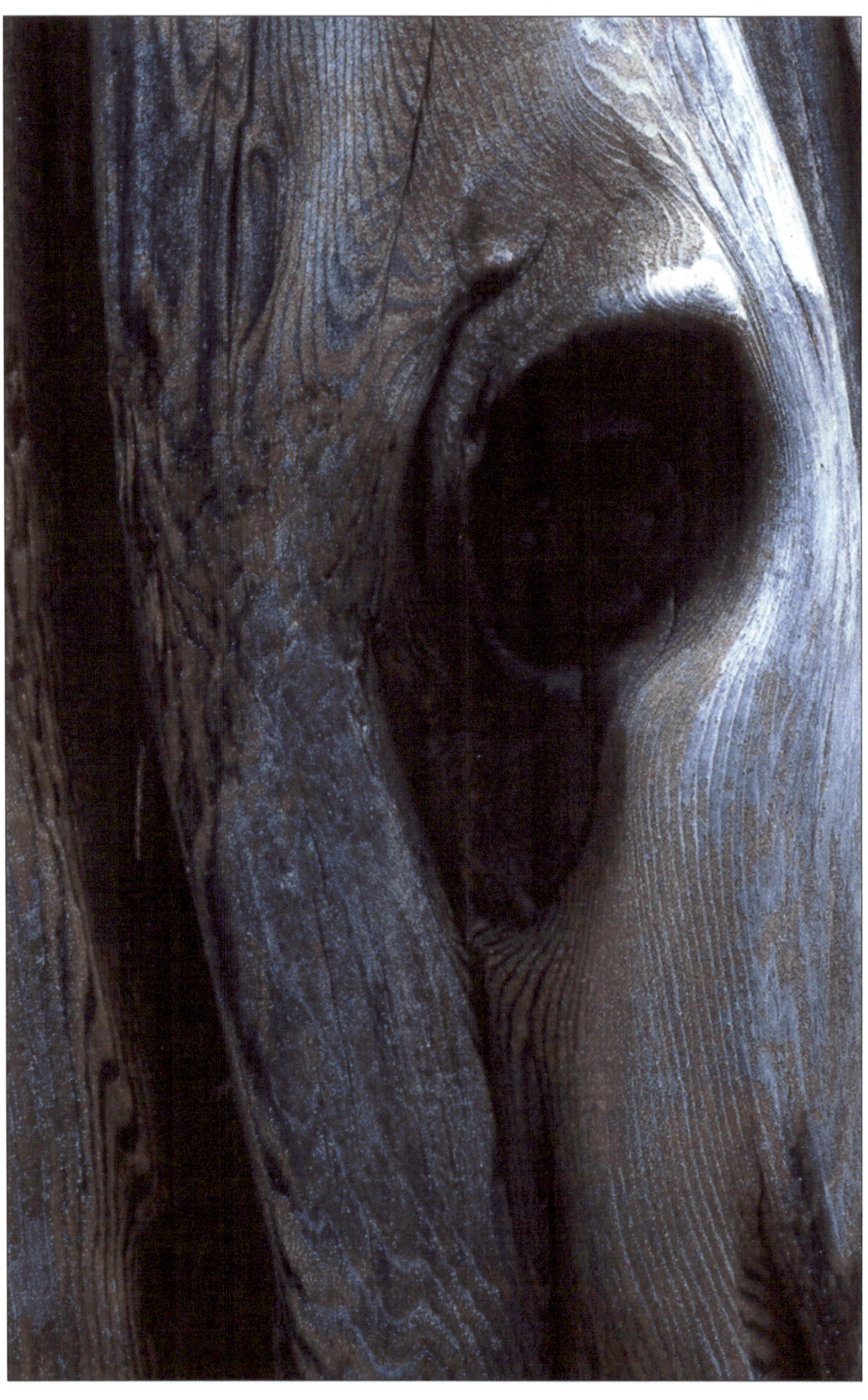

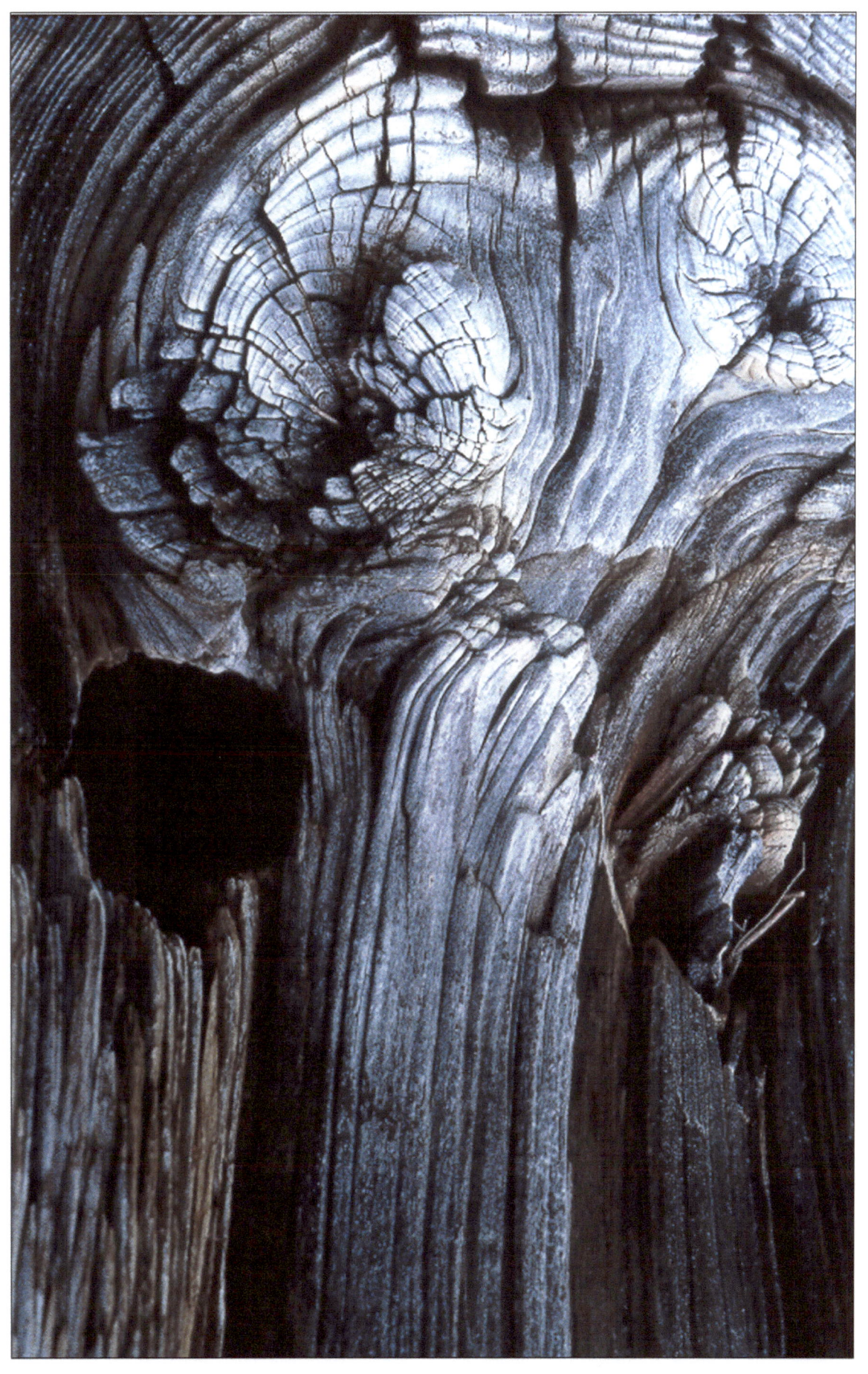

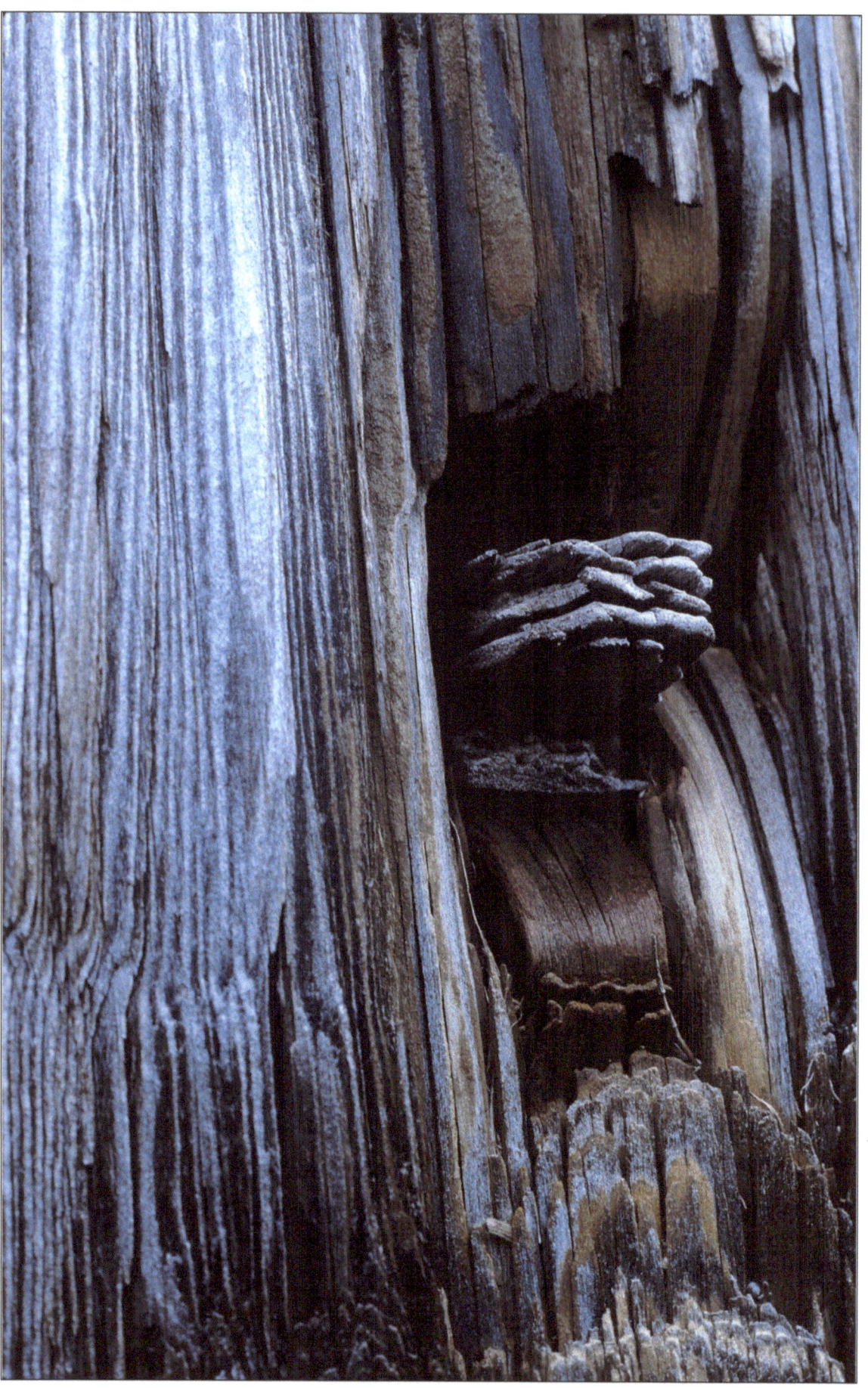

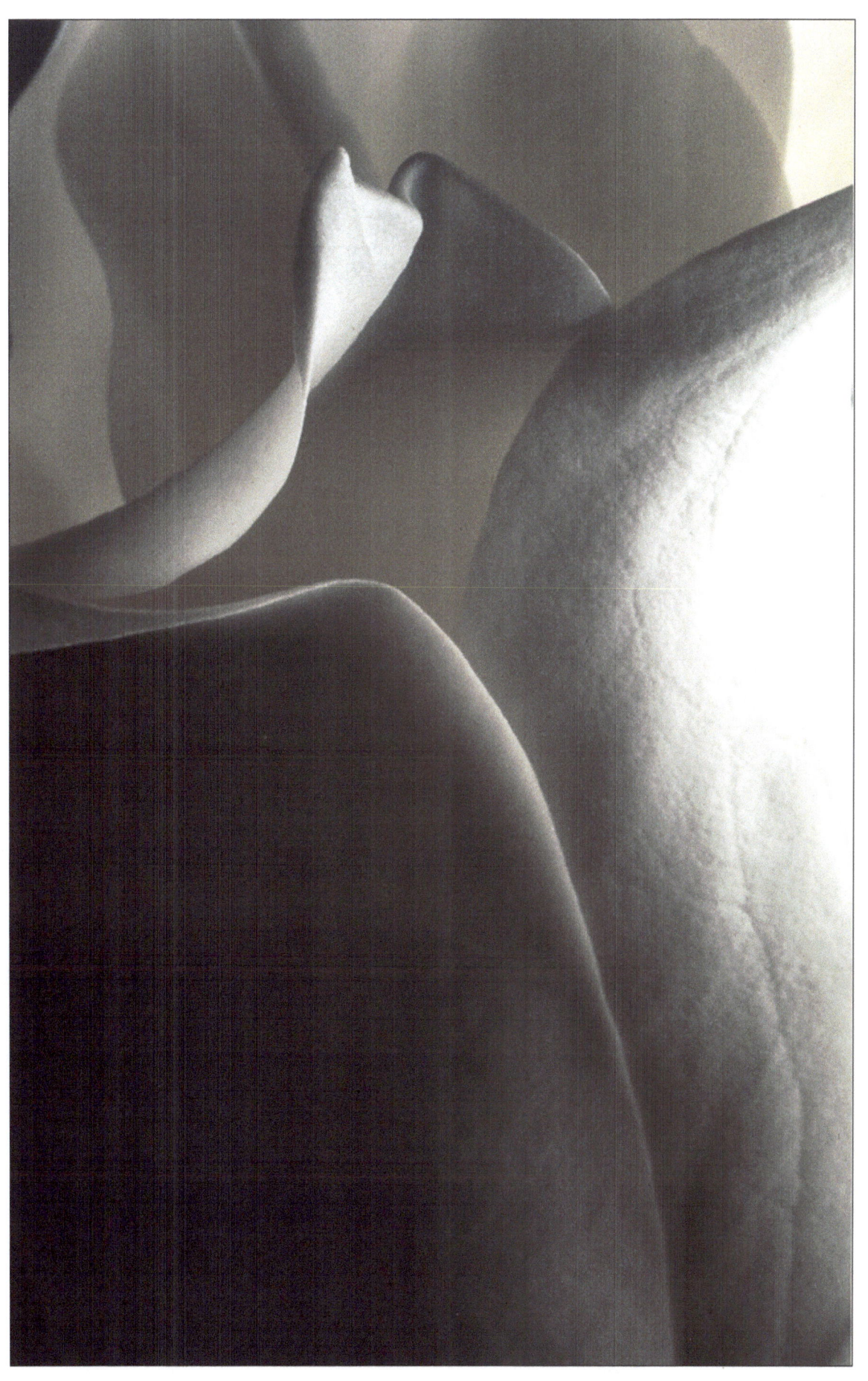

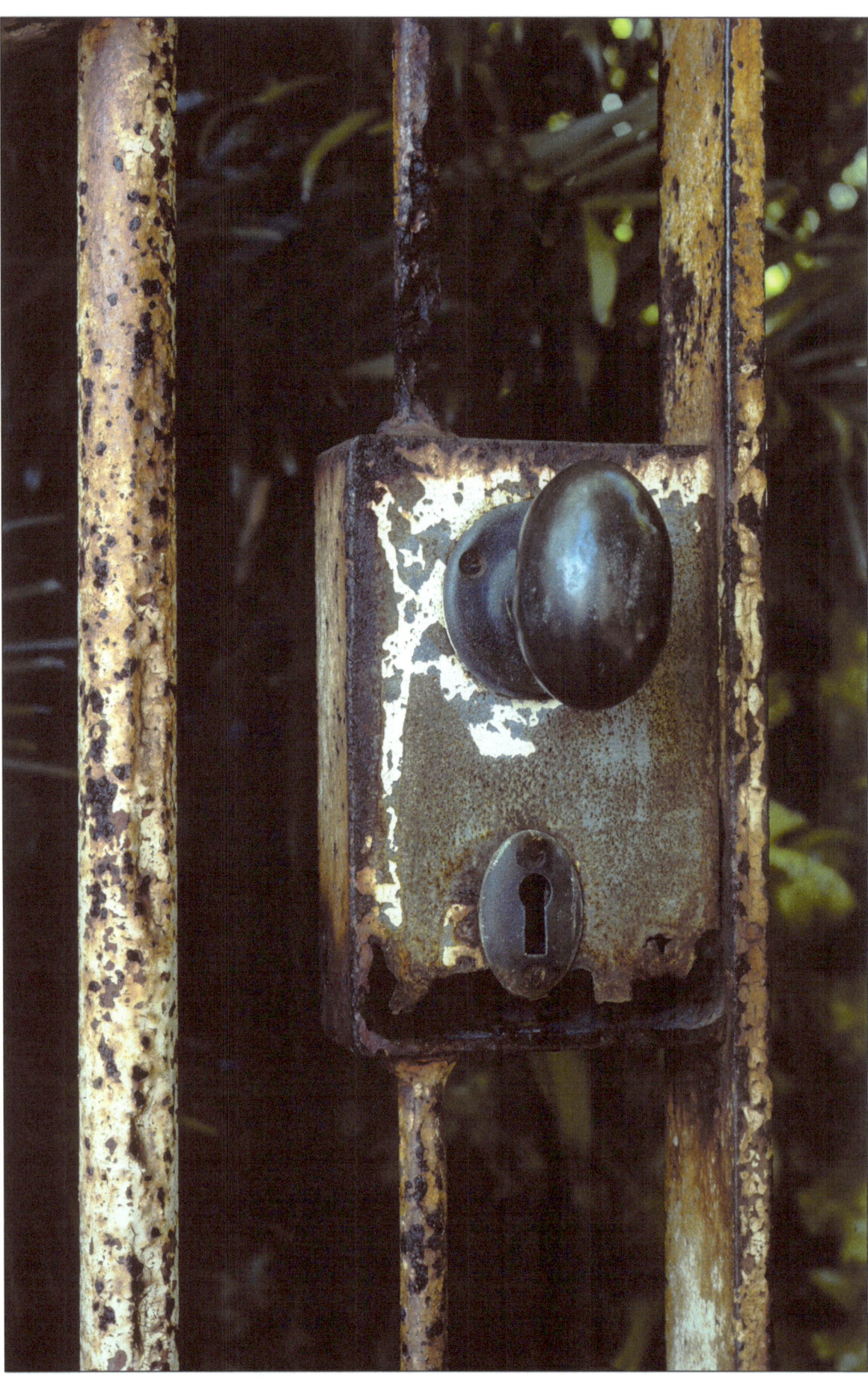

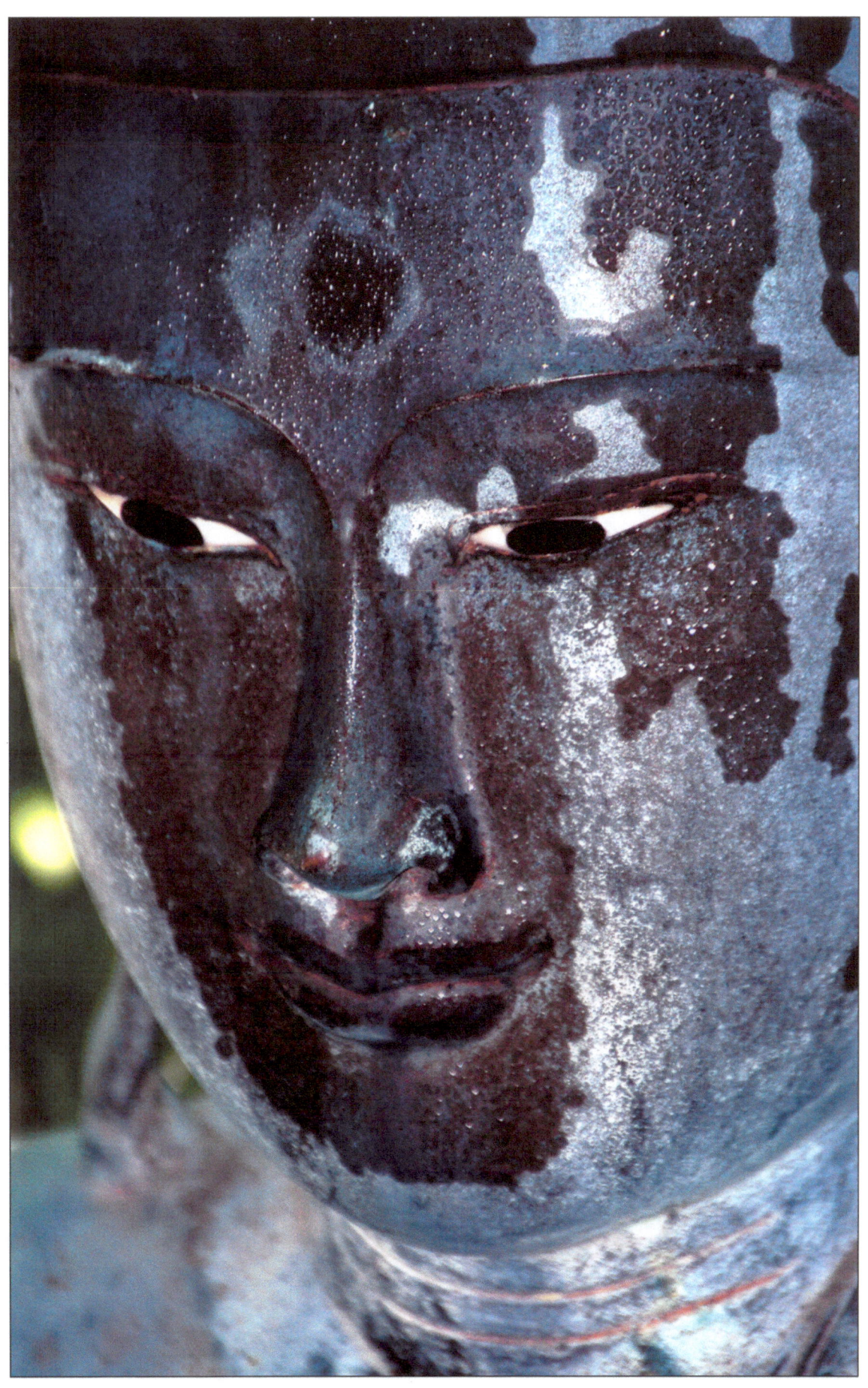

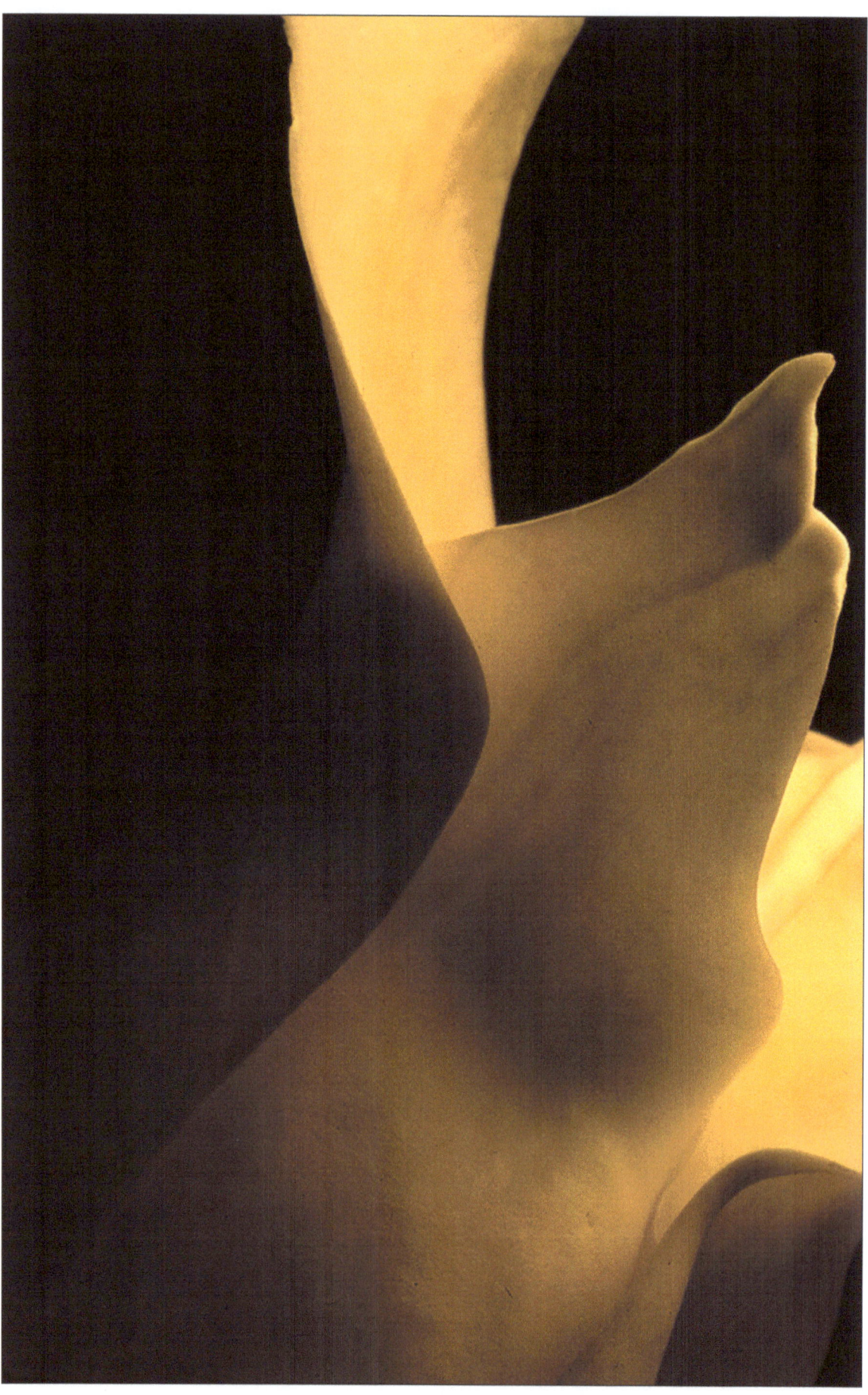

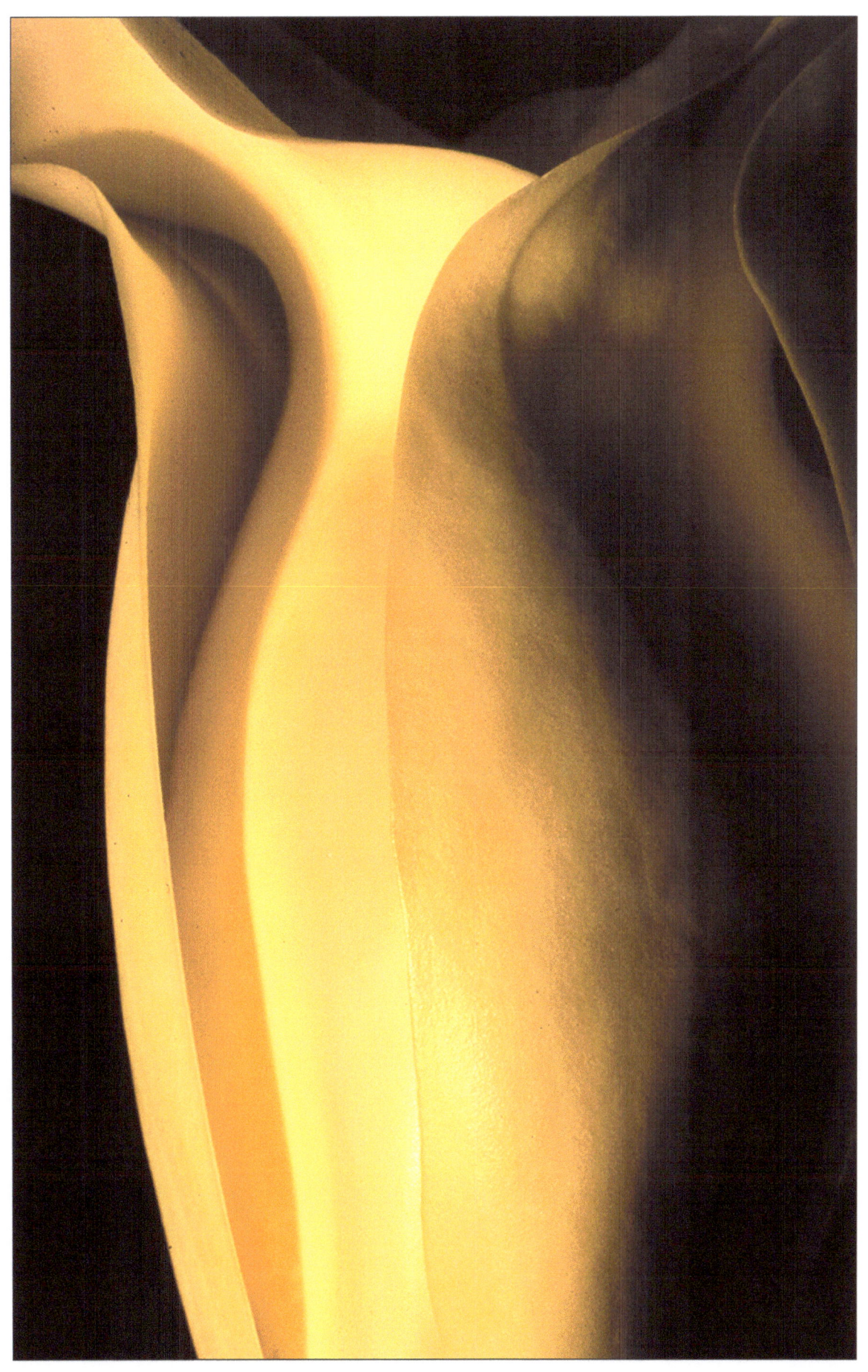

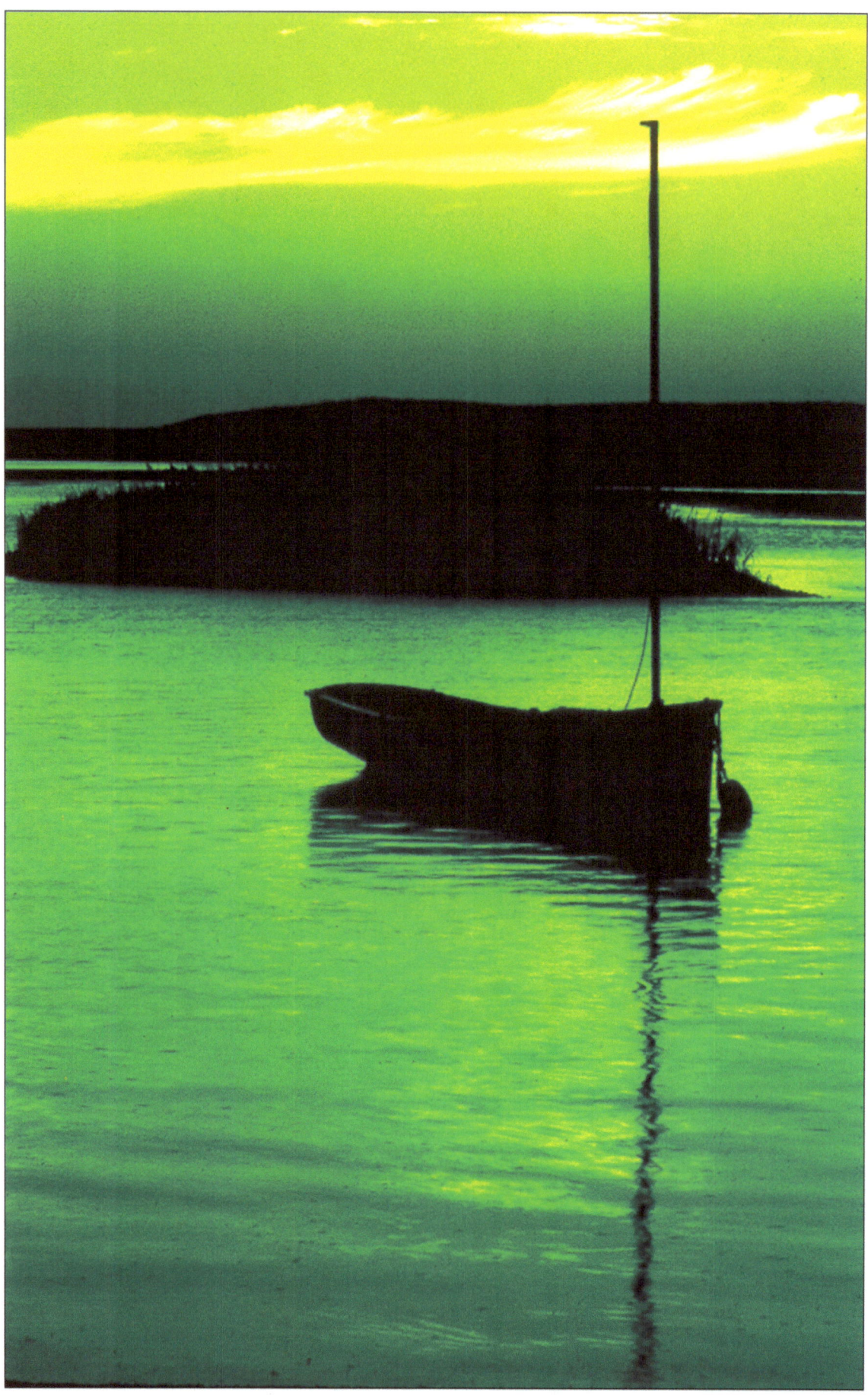

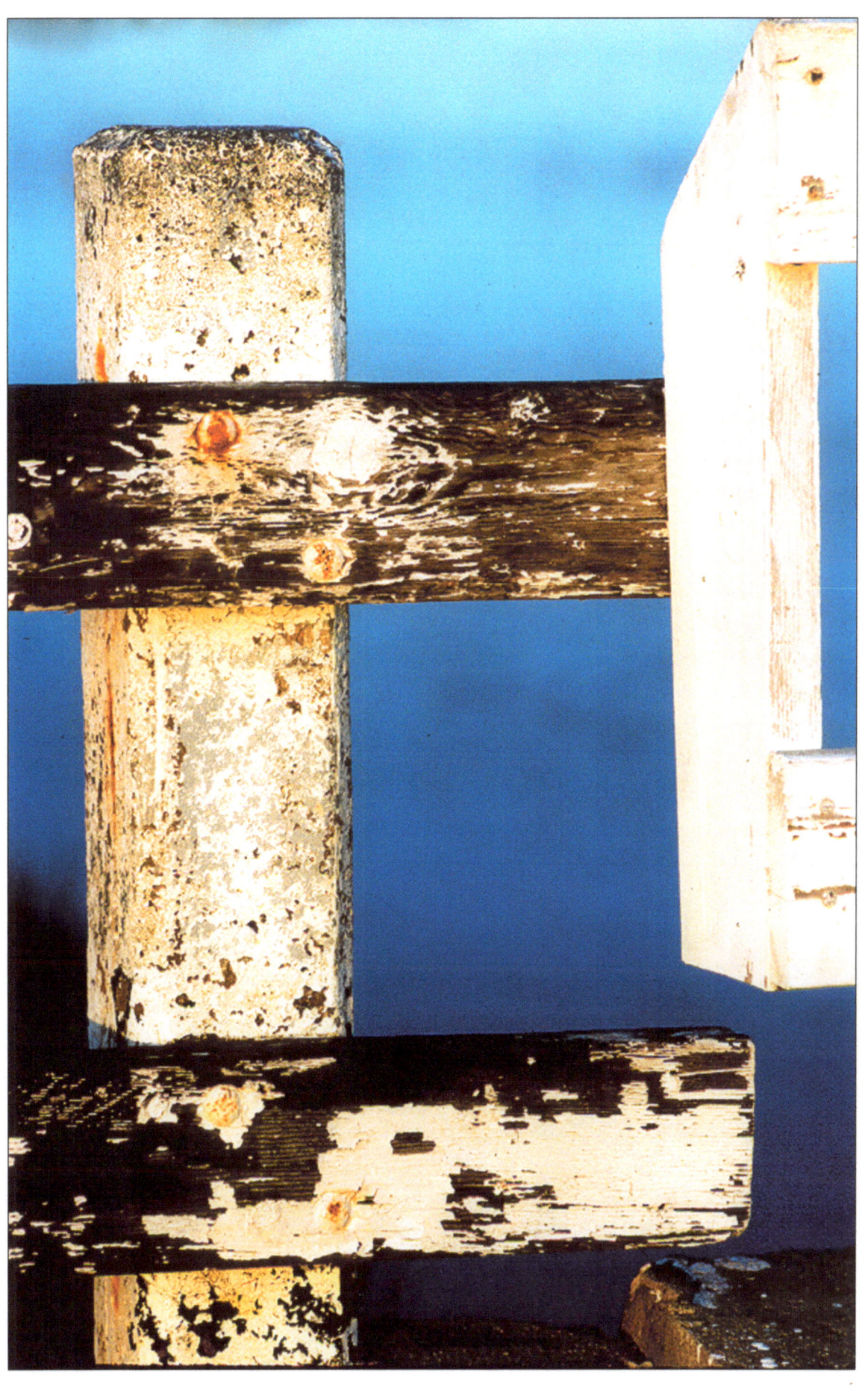

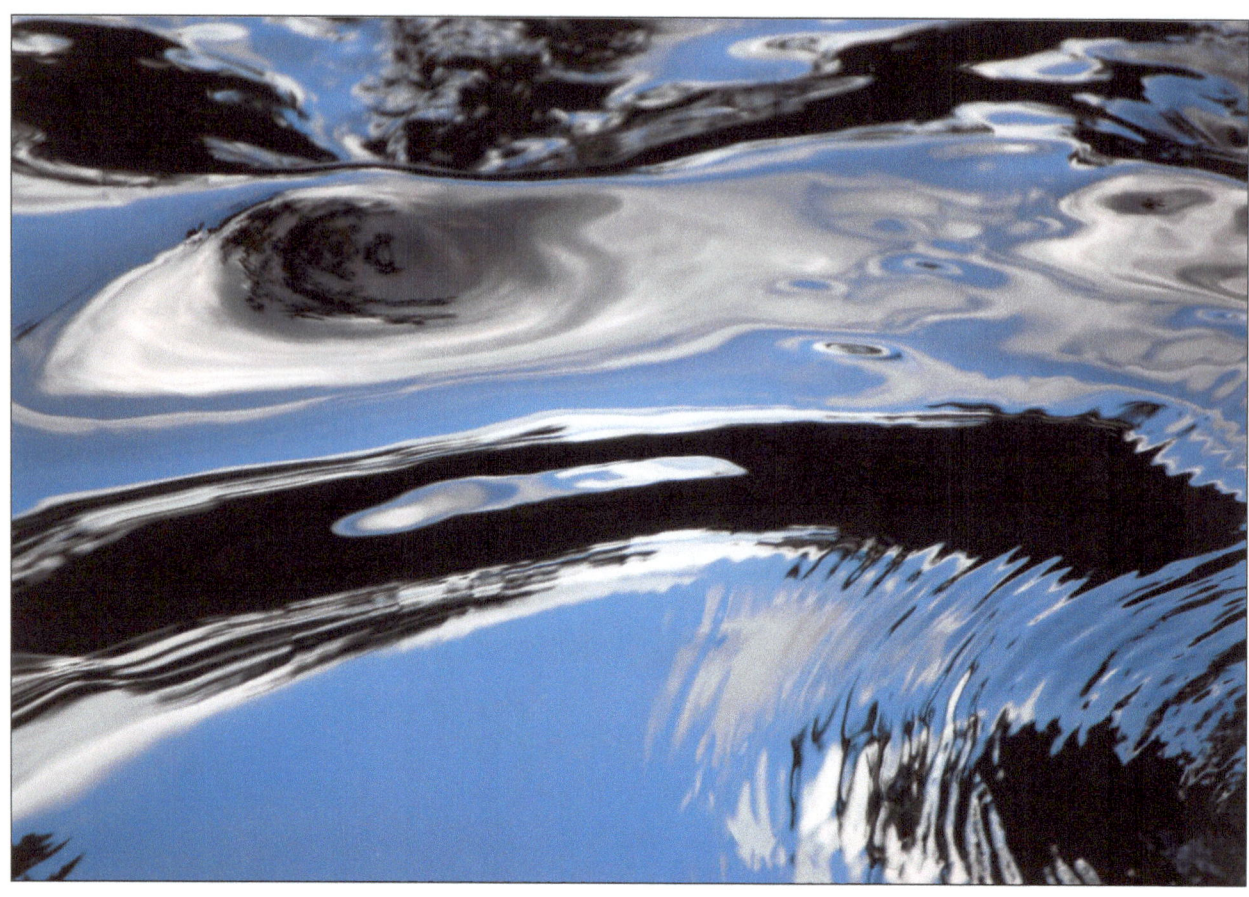

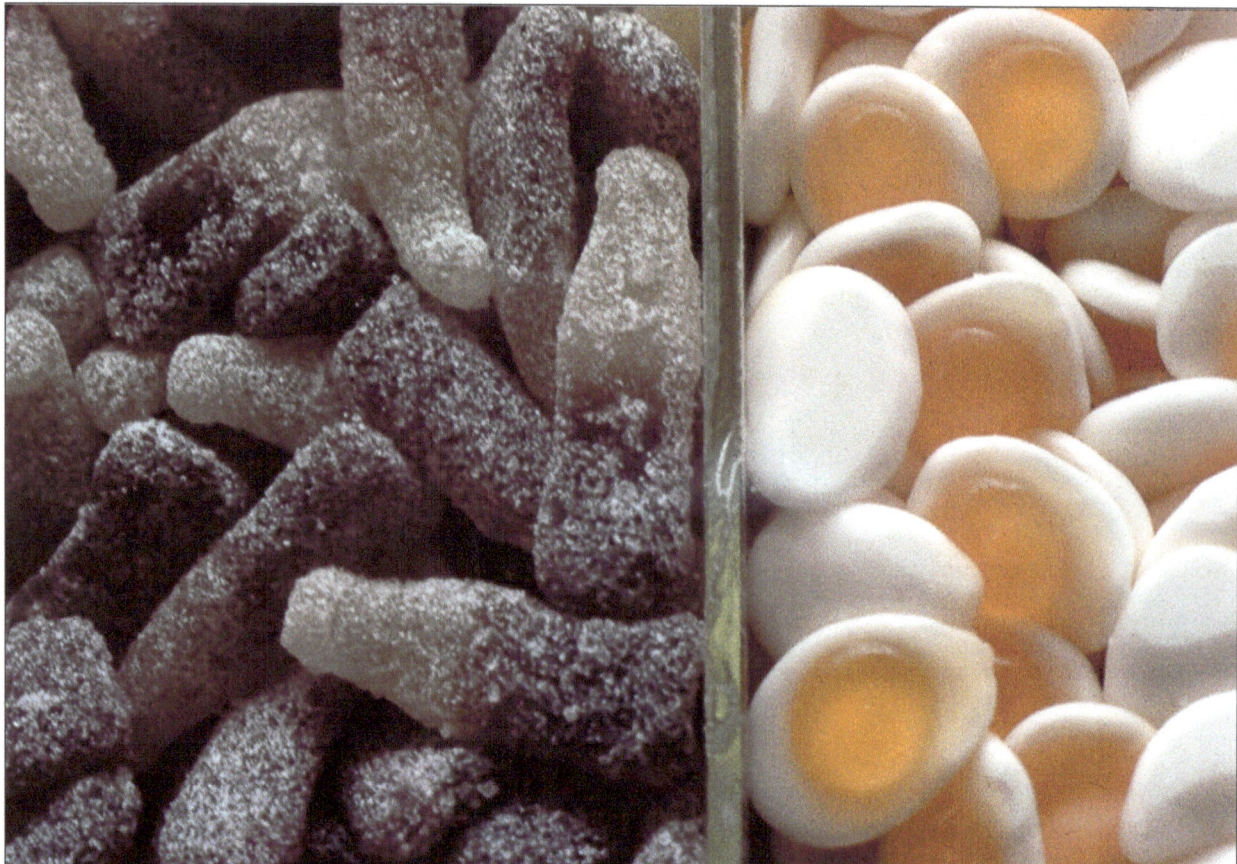

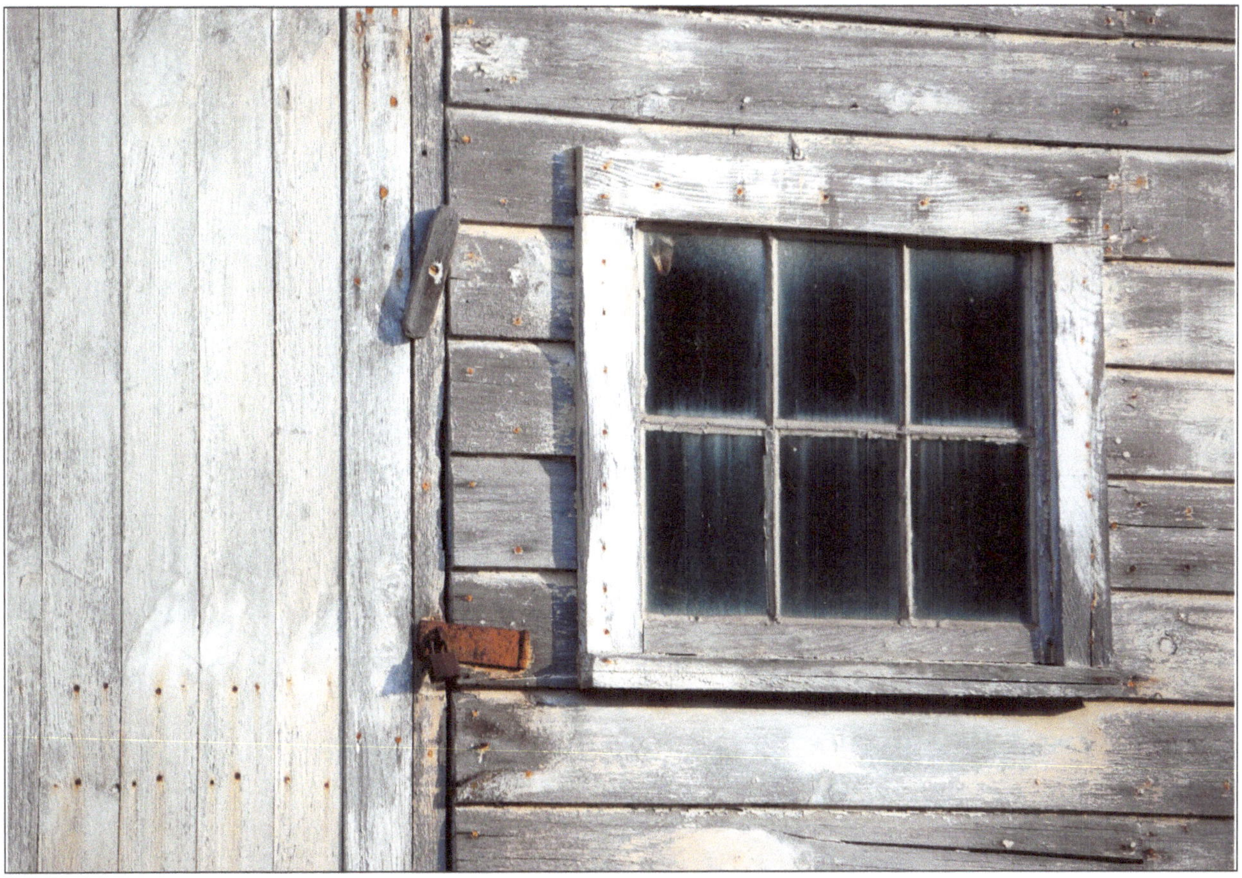

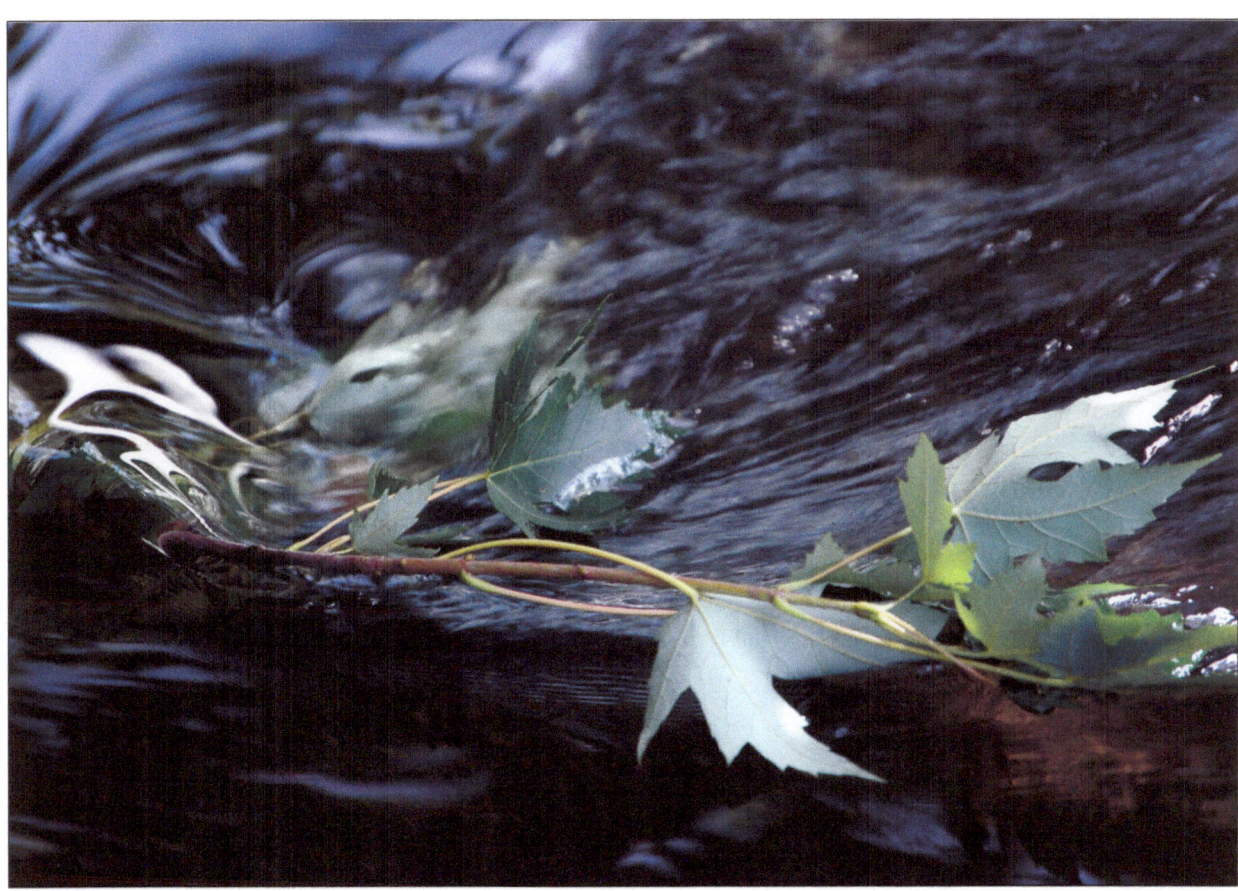

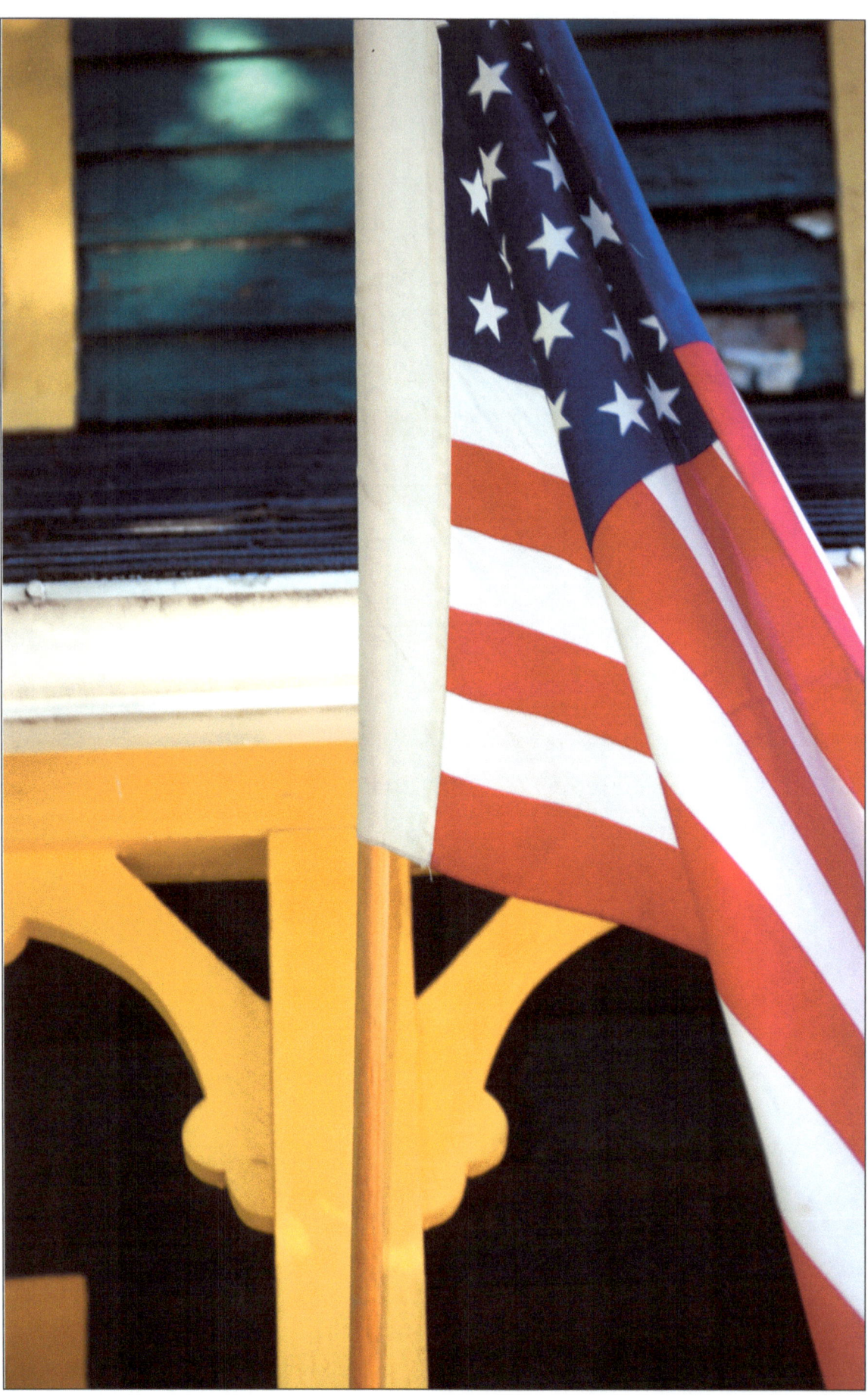

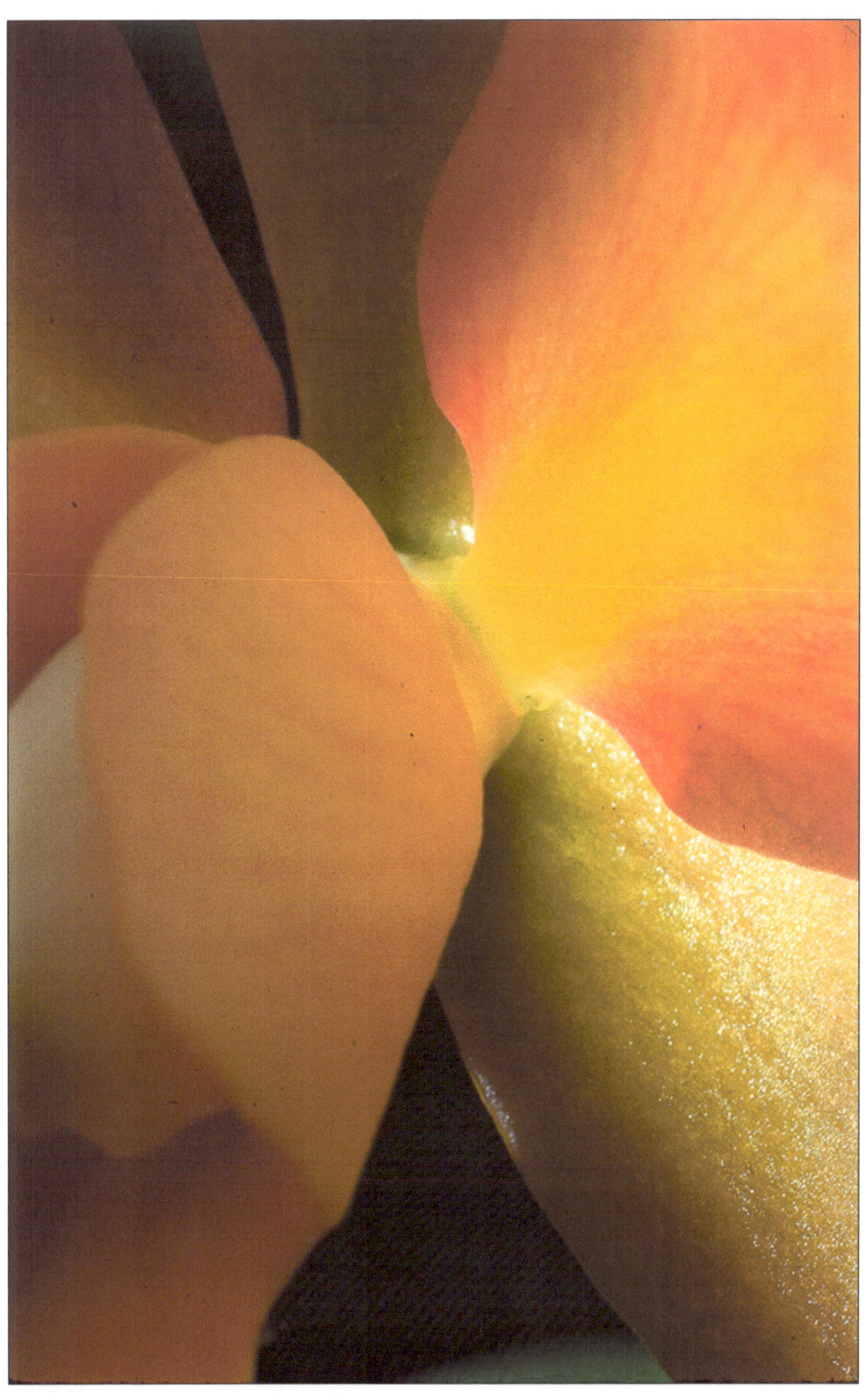

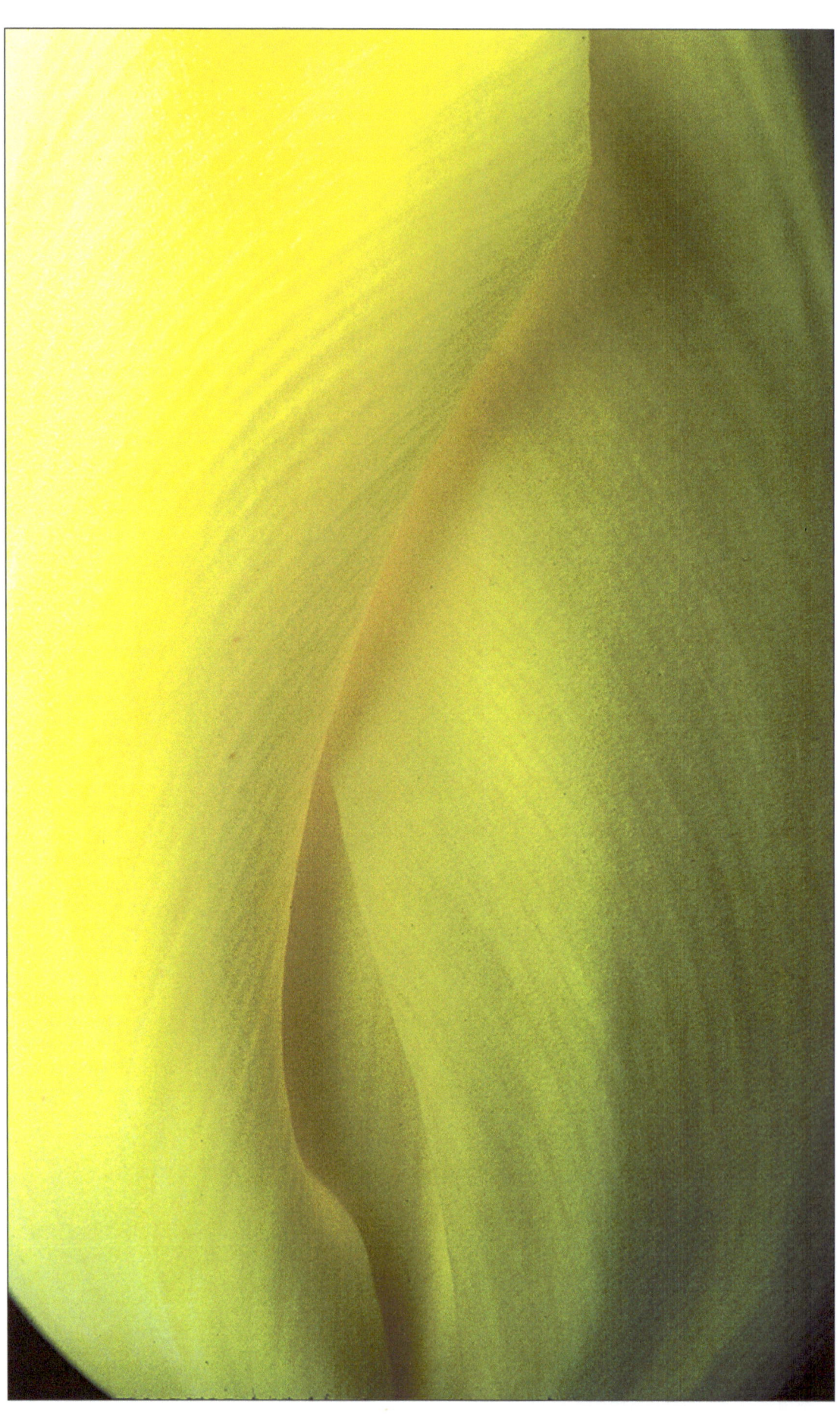

44

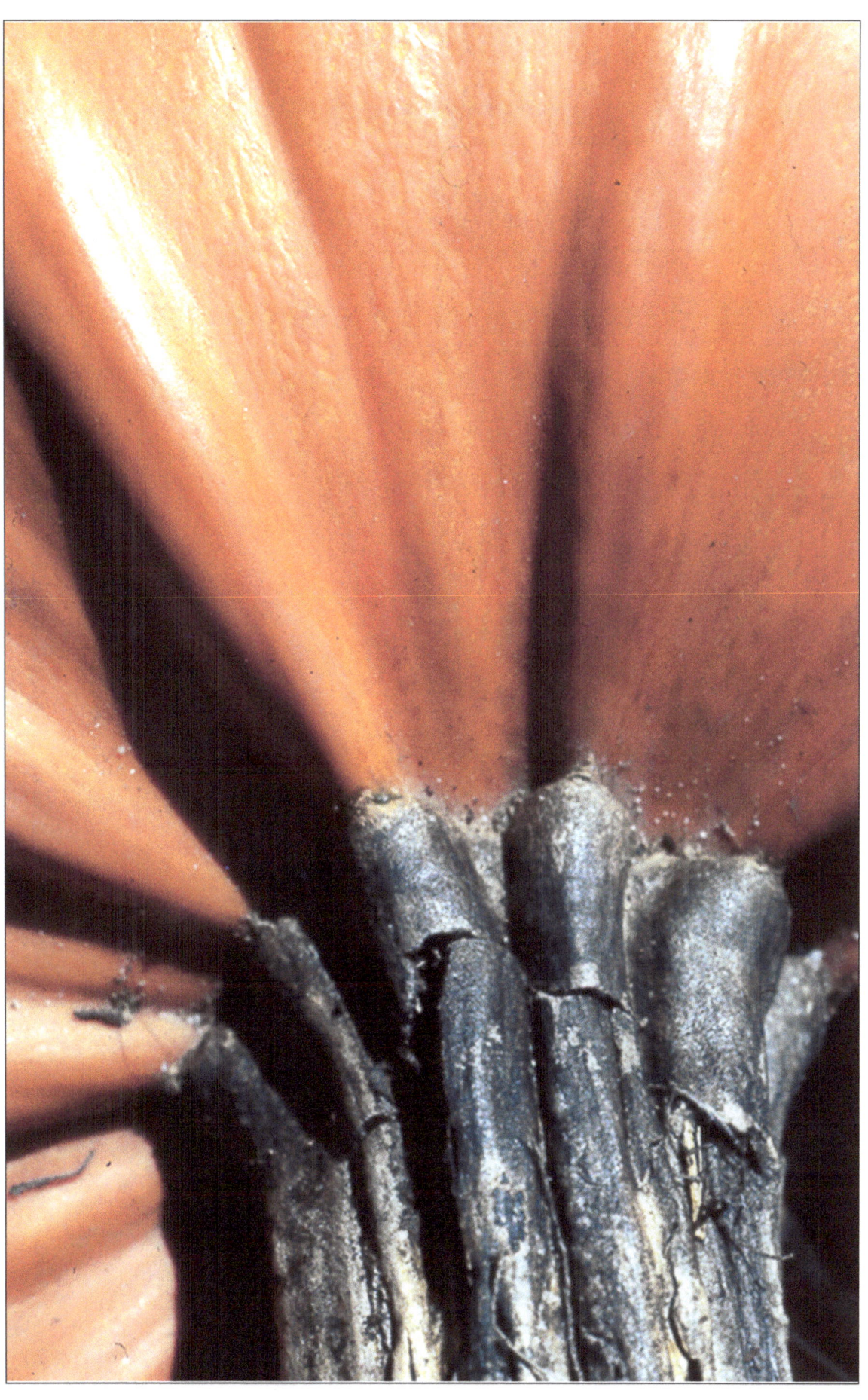

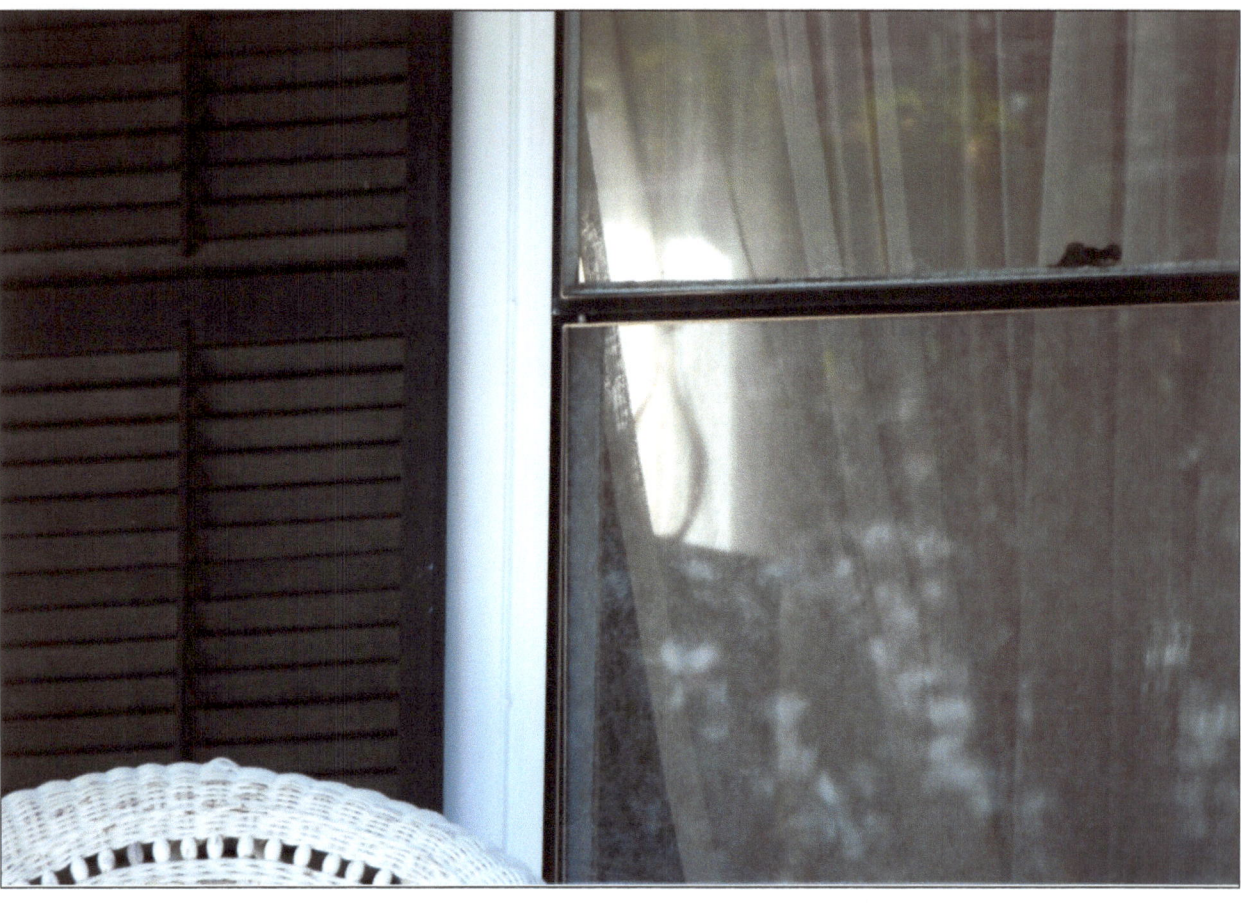

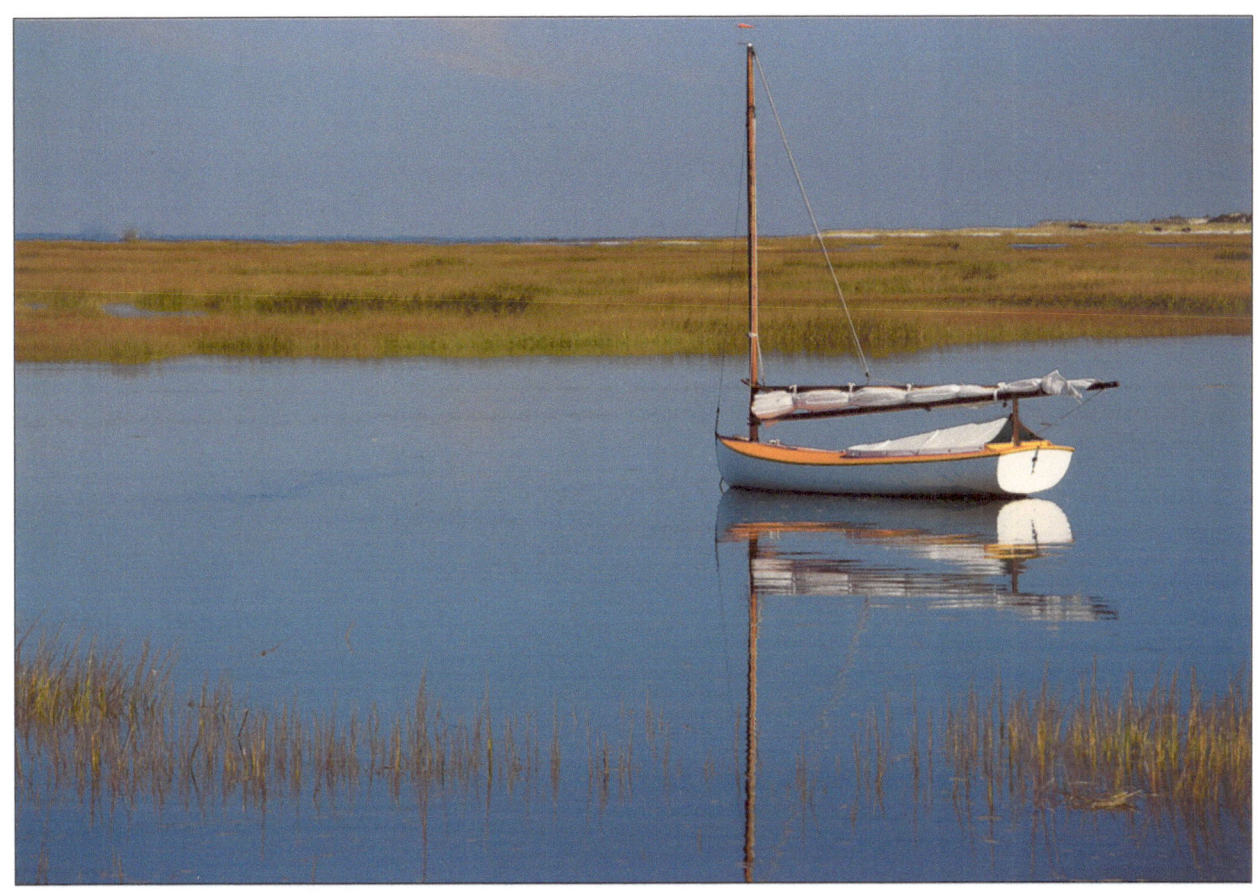

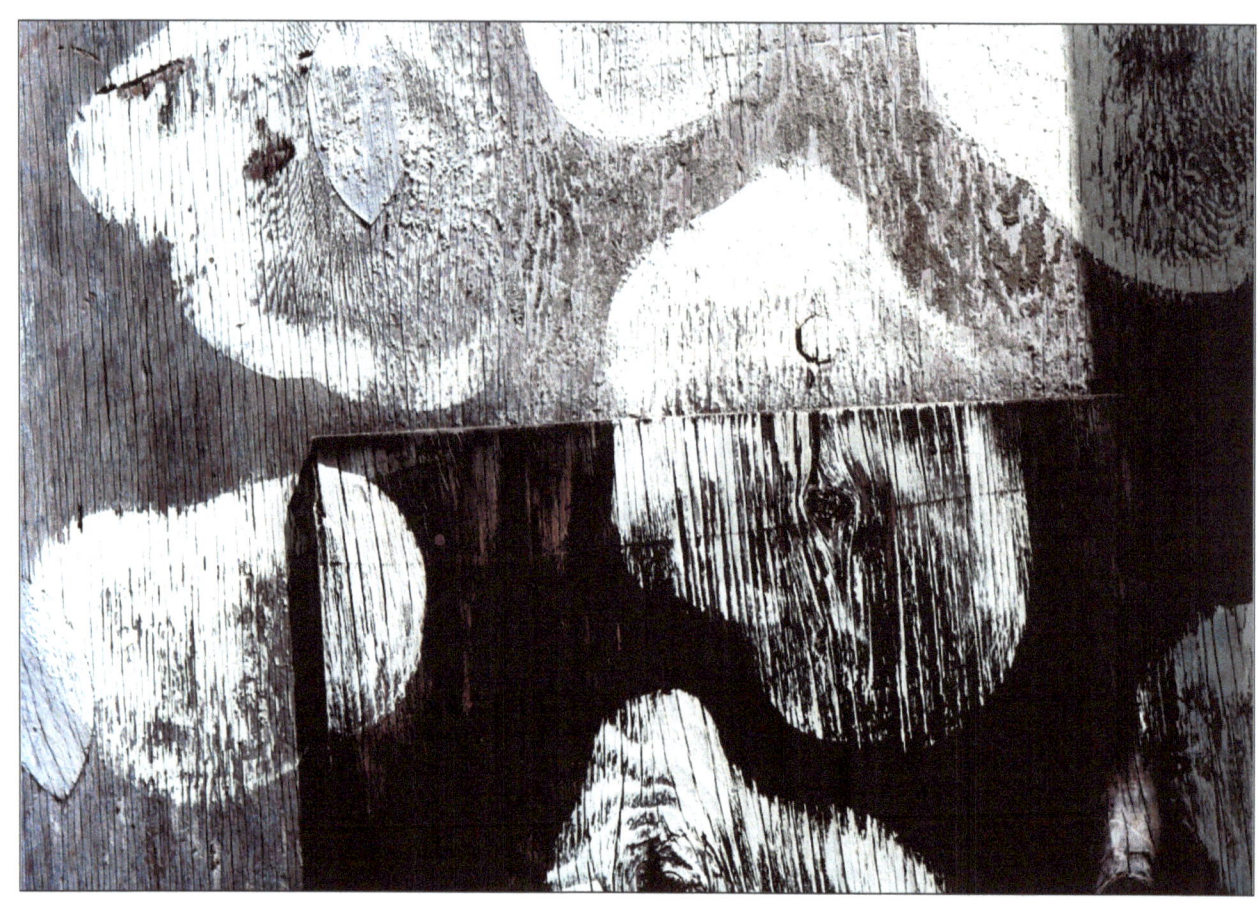

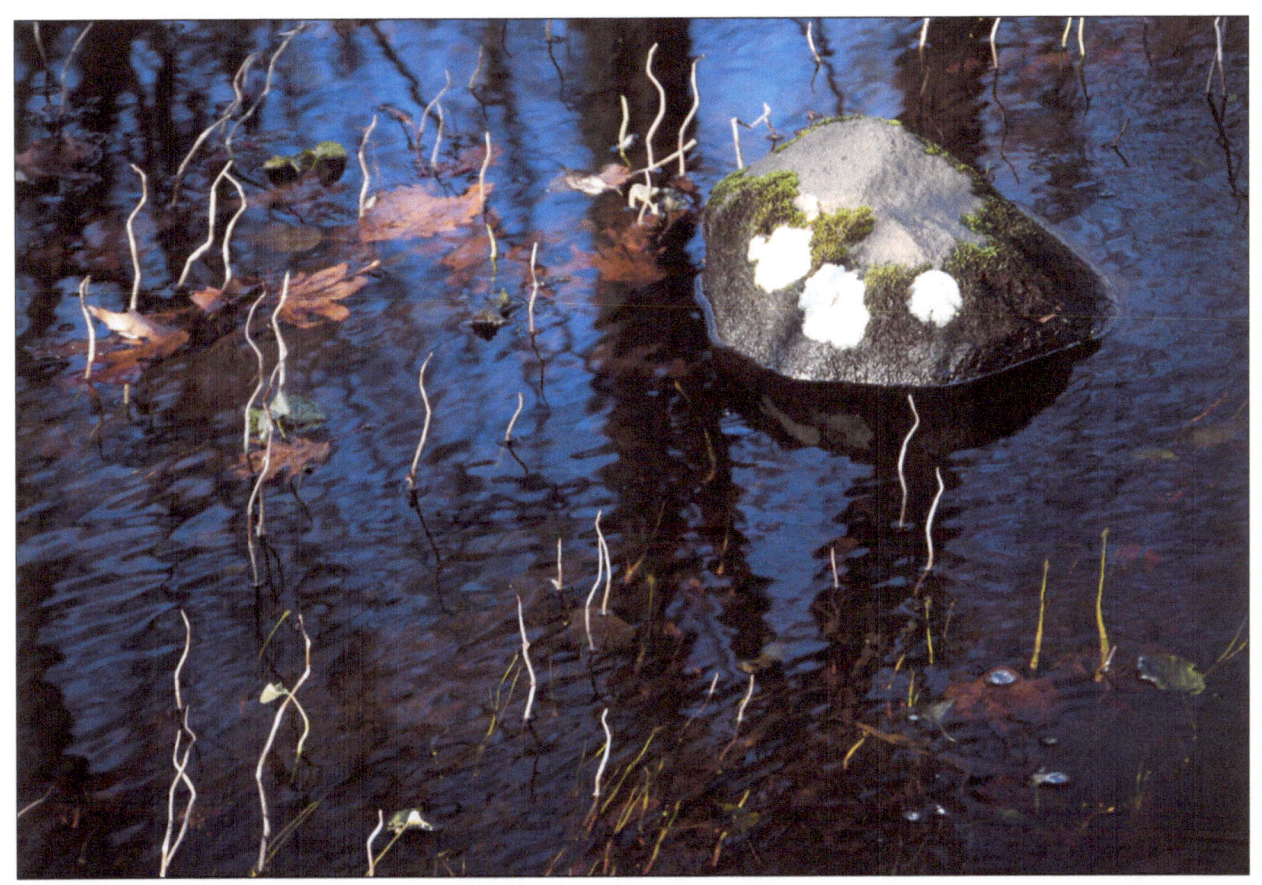

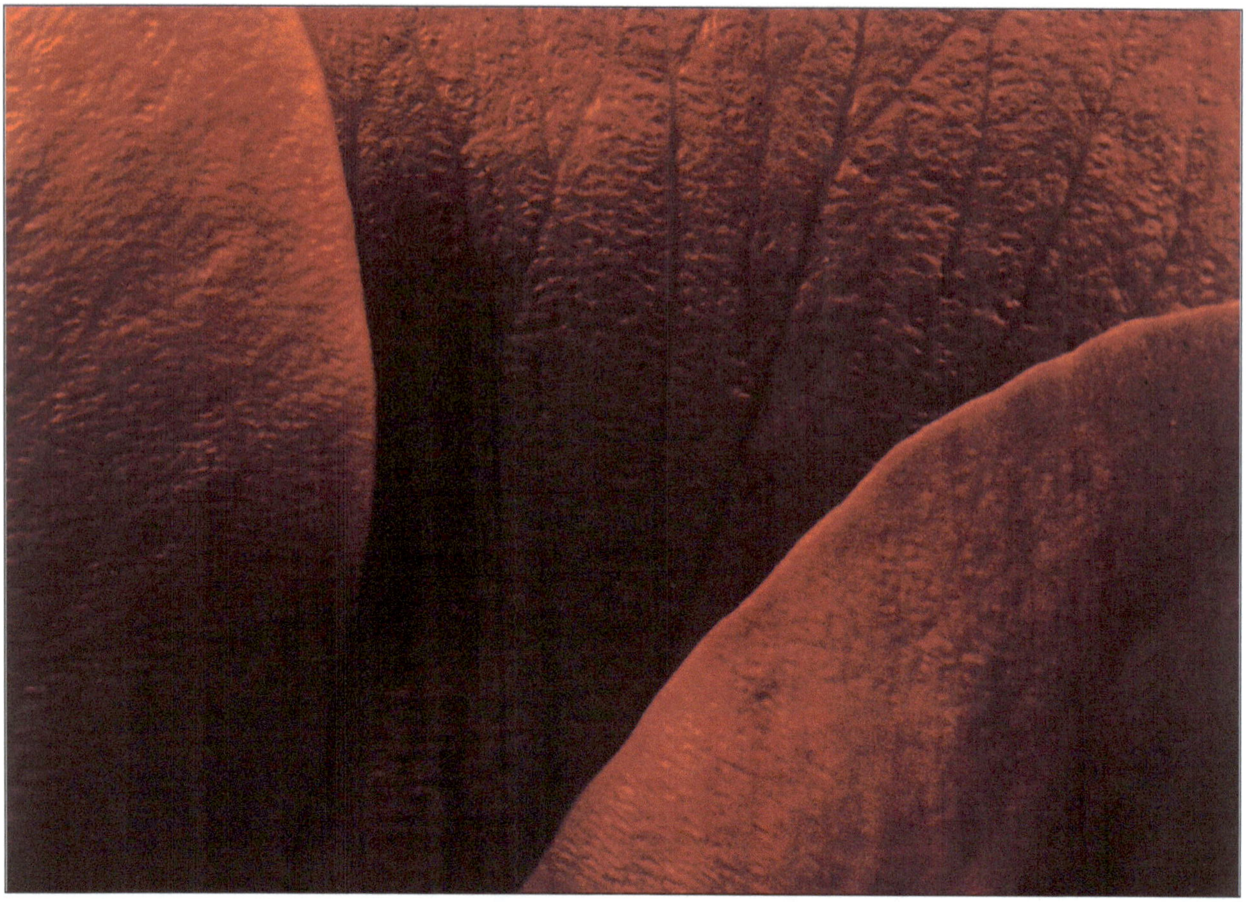

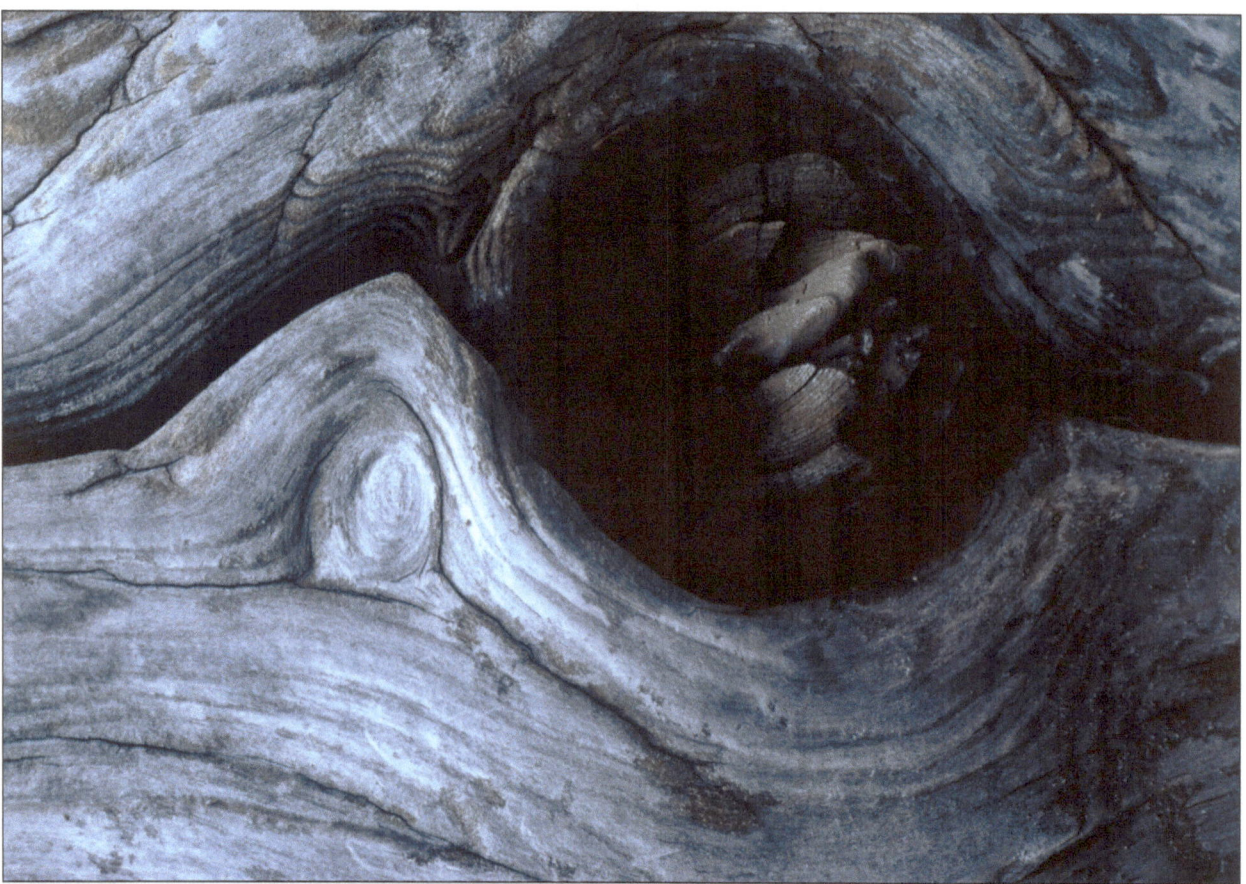

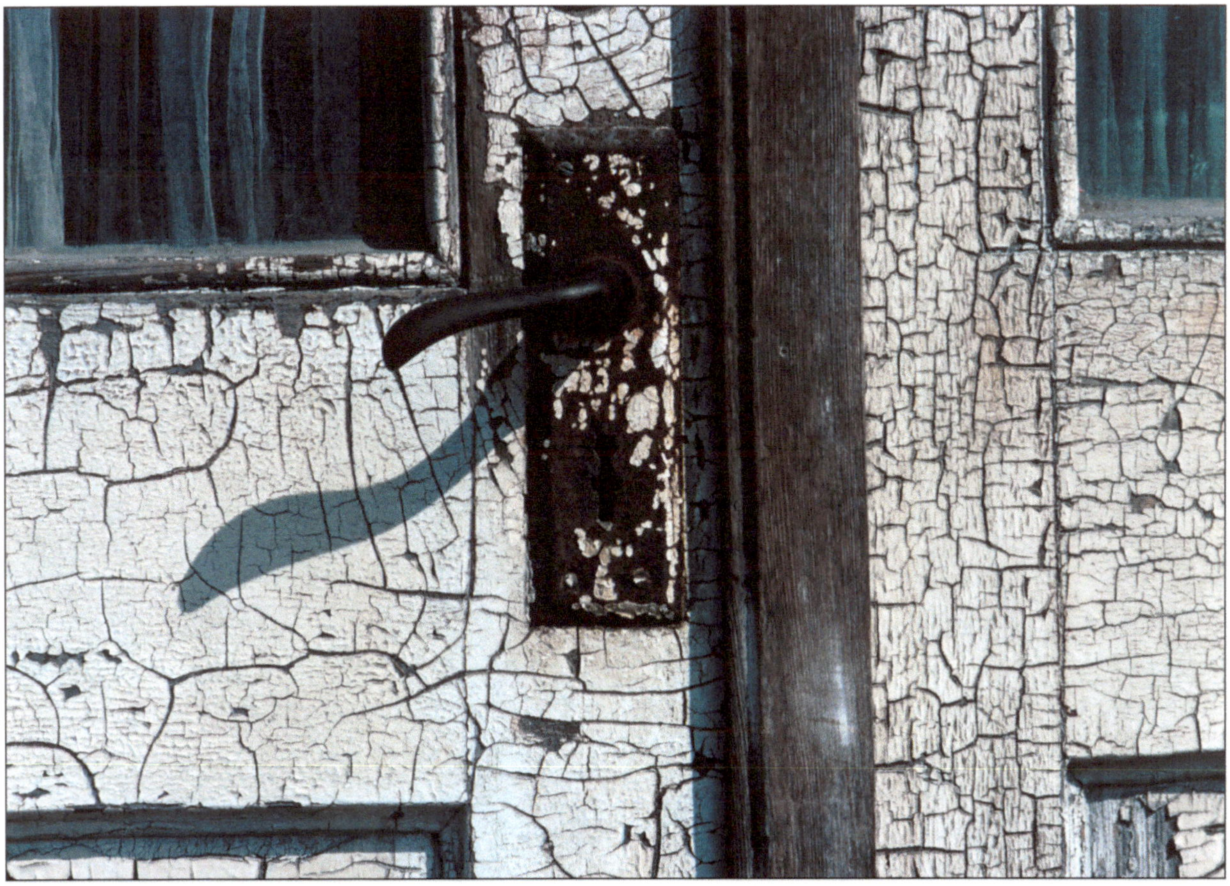

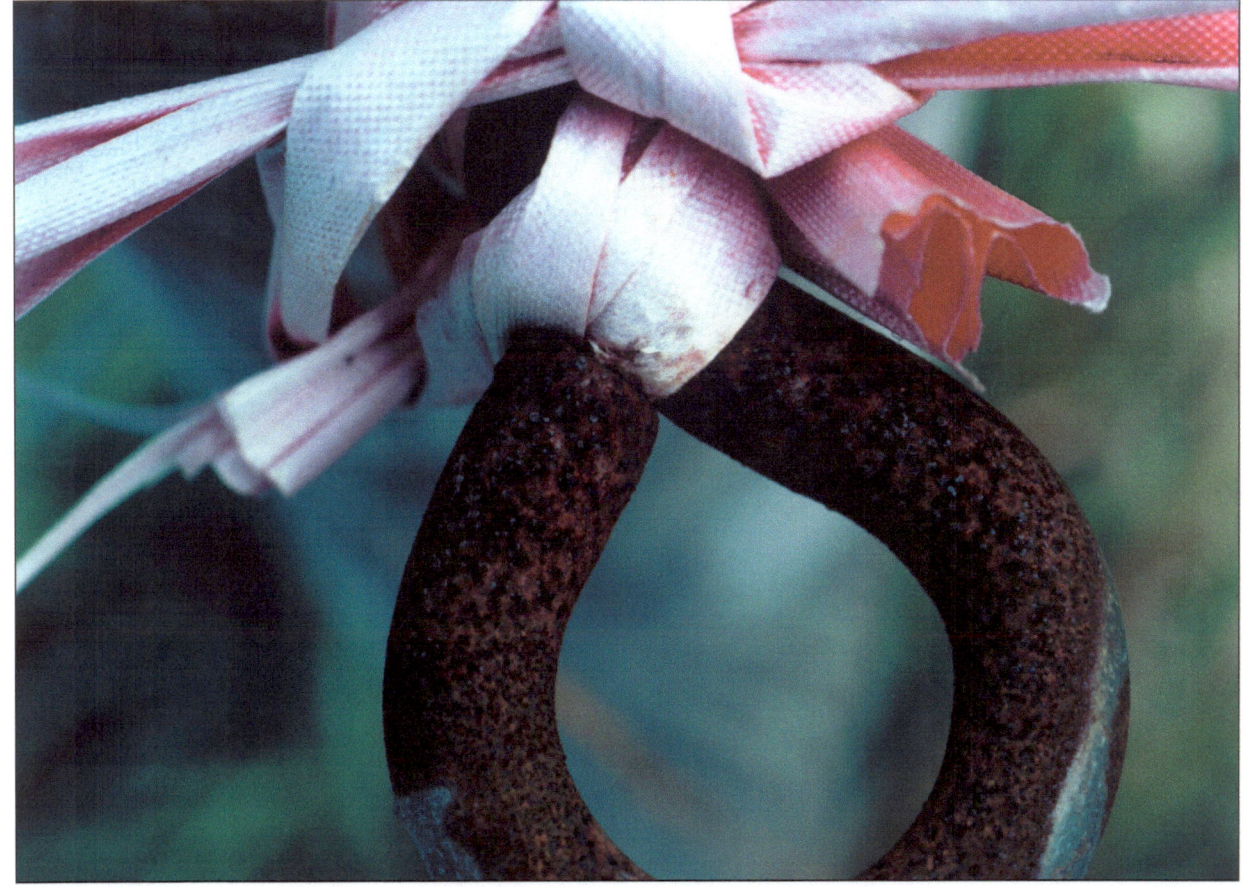

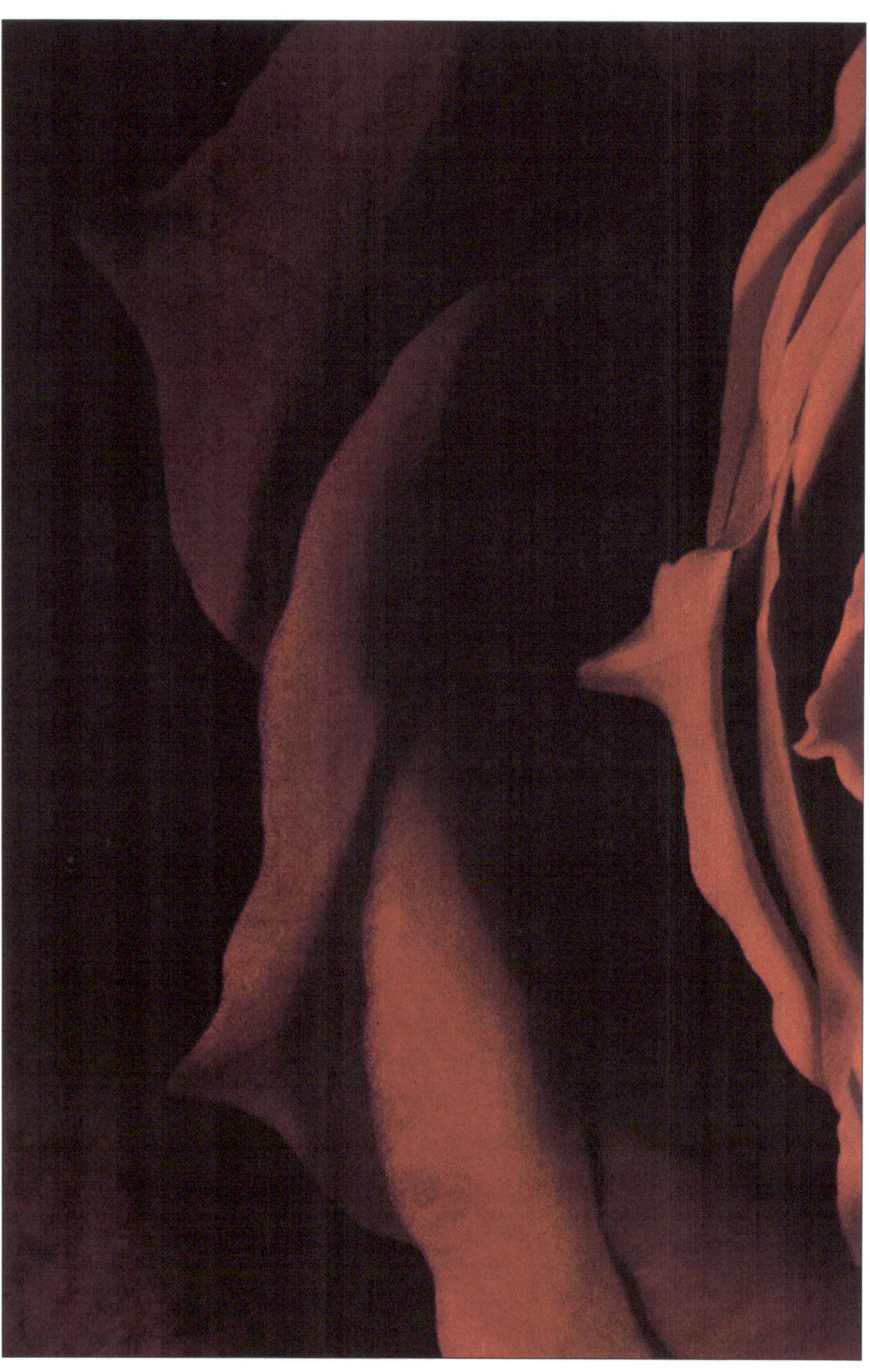

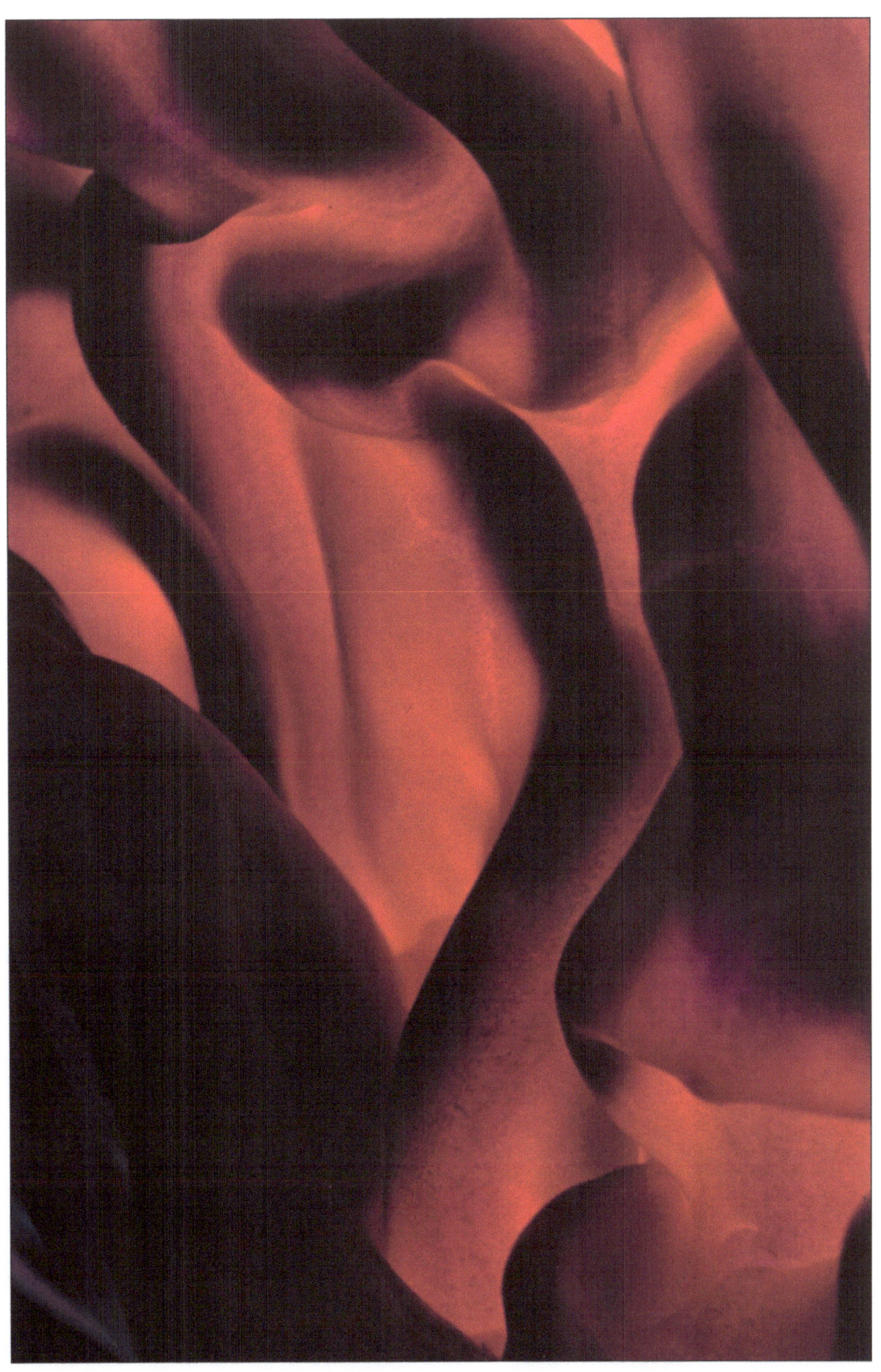

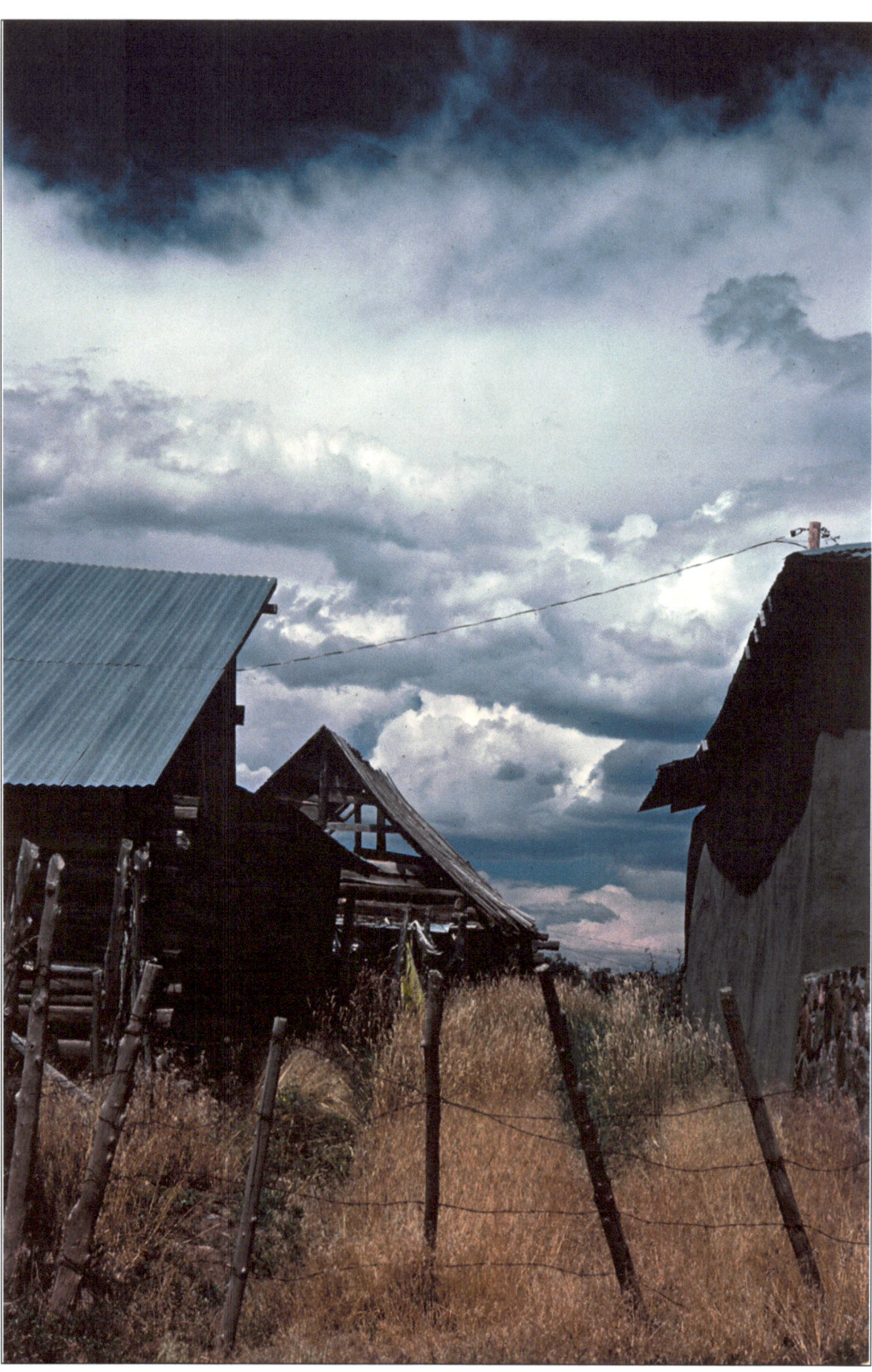

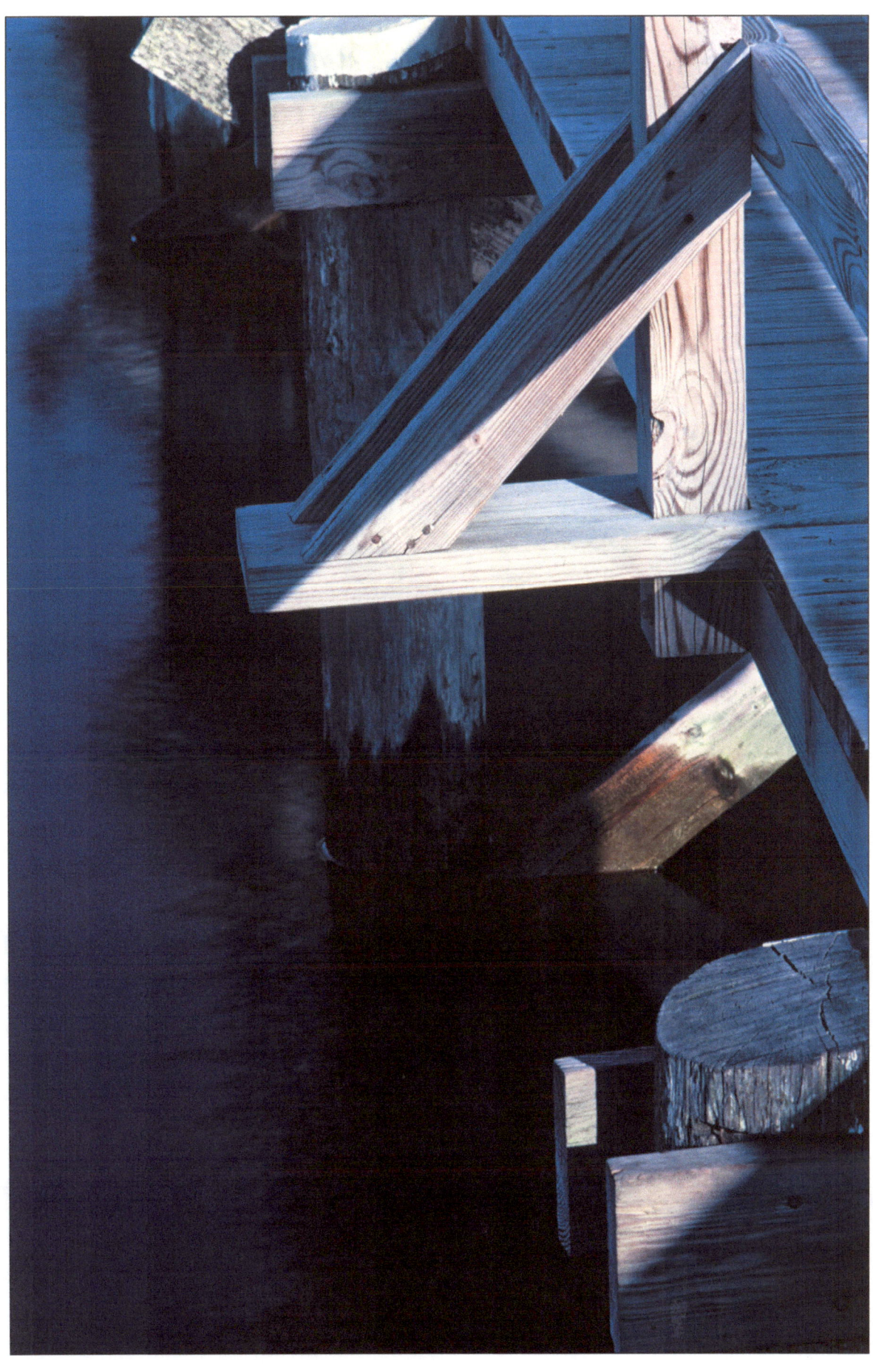

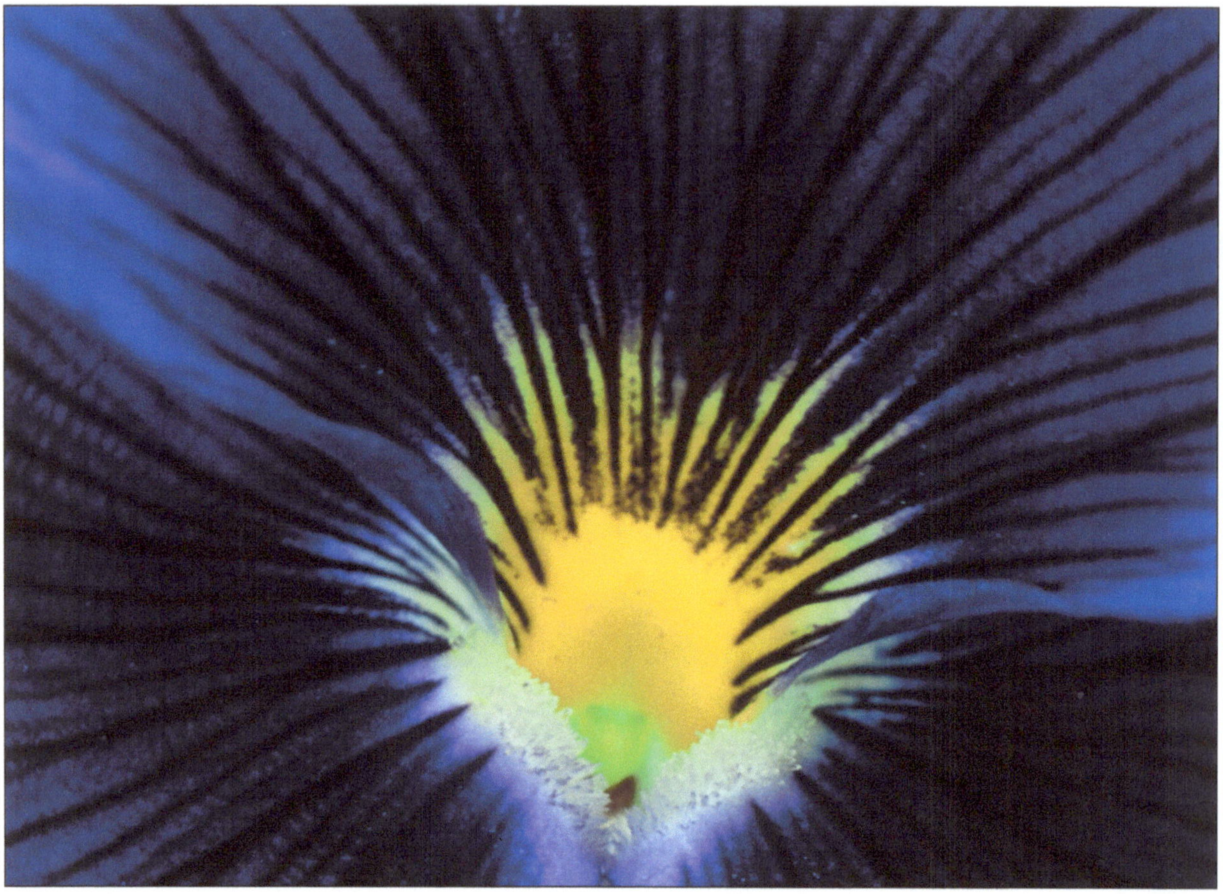

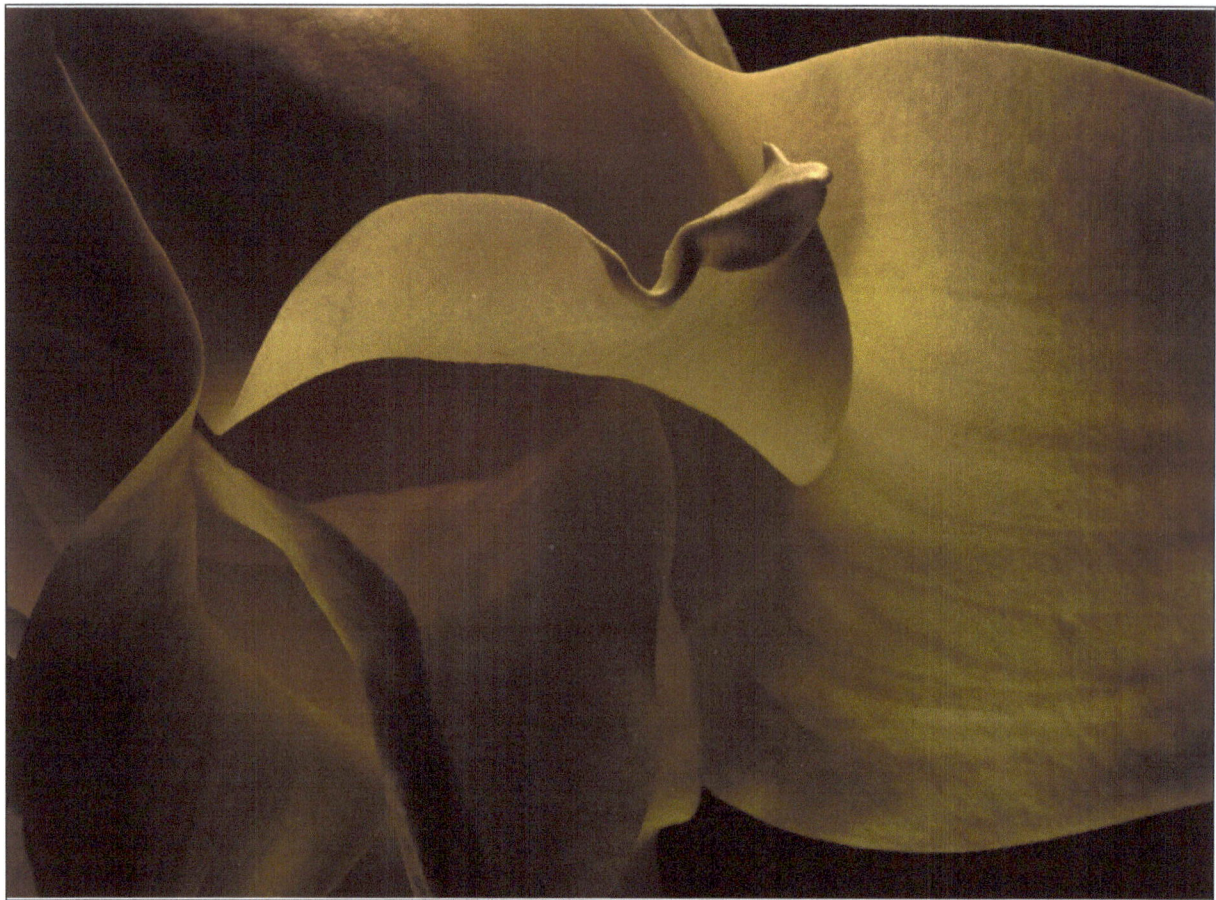

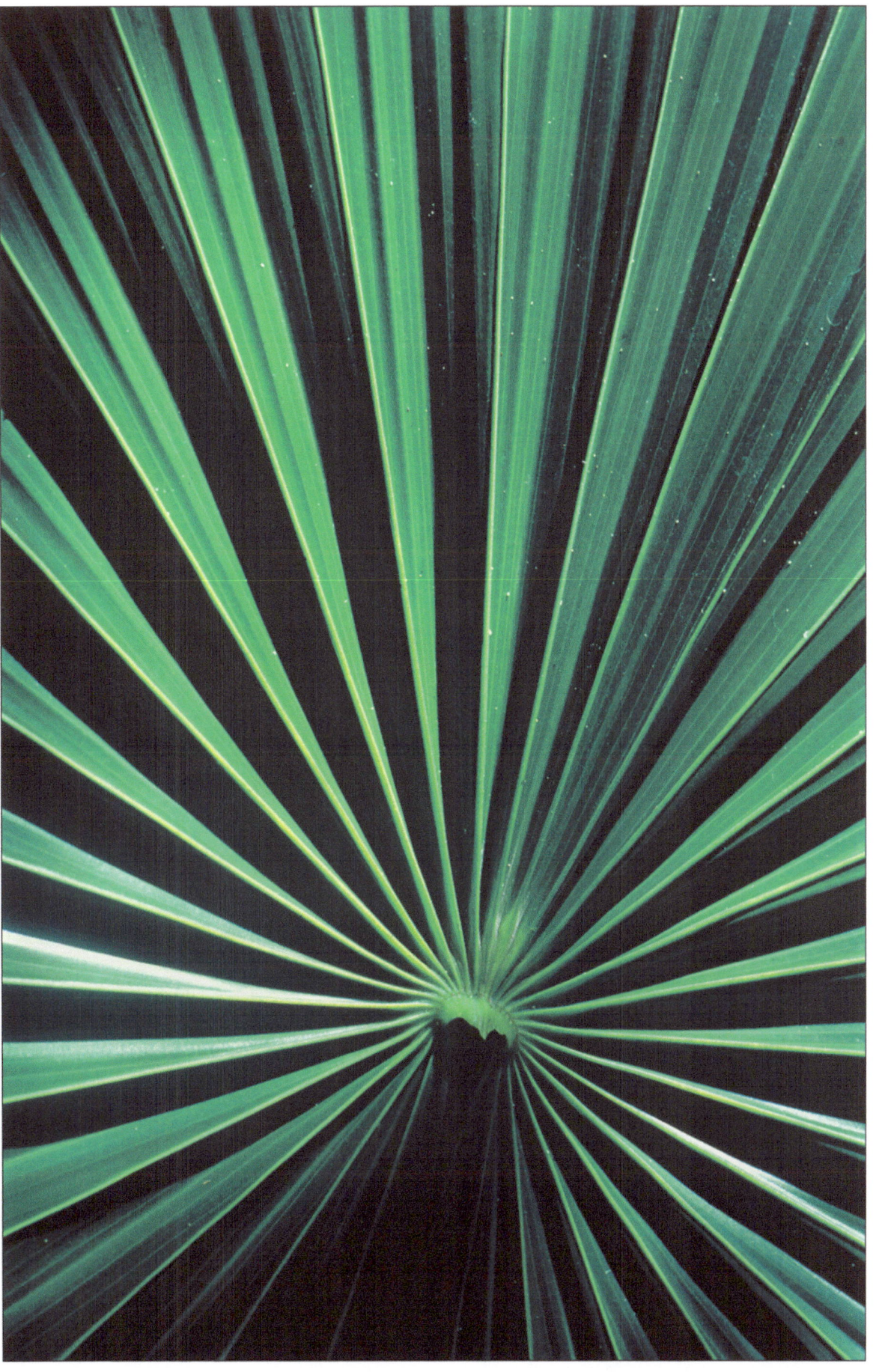

CAPTIONS

Page 1: *Suzy's Breakfast,* 1975. Shot at *f* 32 with a Micro-Nikkor 55mm Macro lens on Kodachrome 25. Just visible in the upper right of the image is a Weber barbecue, at the house in Closter, New Jersey, on which I positioned the subject in order to capture the early-morning light. I can't remember if my daughter subsequently ate the subject.

Page 2: *Barn Door Brace, Margaretville, NY,* 2006. Shot at *f* 8 with a Nikkor Zoom 85-200 mm lens and polarizing filter. The abrasion, which looks like a missing spring, haunted me like an amputated limb.

Page 3: *Ramondskill Falls, Milford, PA,* 2010. Shot at *f* 22, 1/15th sec., with a Nikkor Zoom 85-200 and a polarizing filter. The falls were in full spring flood. I was trying to find local images for a show Fran Wood was mounting for me at Patina and Company's Broad Street store in Milford. I had to slightly alter the gamma to retain texture in the brightest white.

Page 4 (Above): *Flag Abstraction, Jacques Marchais Museum, Staten Island, NY,* 2006. Shot at *f* 5.6 with a 60mm Nikkor. The Marchais houses a superb collection of Tibetan art. The color values of the prayer flags struck me.

Page 4 (Below): *Flower Abstraction, Sandwich, MA,* 2006. Six months separated this image from the previous one. The flowers were still blooming, but they were covered in plastic wrap against the October chill.

Page 5: *House, La Boca, Buenos Aires, Argentina,* 2007. Most of the houses in the port section of town are painted like this. Shot at *f* 22 with my son's zoom Nikkor.

Page 6: *Gravestone, Newfane, VT,* 1993. The pearly Vermont morning light, after a night of rain, made this illusion possible—*f* 32 on Ektachrome 64.

Page 7: *The Human Condition,* 1976. Part of a ship's rigging, Kennebunkport, ME. Shot at *f* 8 on Kodachrome 25.

Page 8: *Water Study, Beacon, NY,* 2008. The dam there is a wonder in all weathers. Shot at 1/30th sec. with a Nikkor Zoom 85-200 and a polarizing filter.

Page 9 (Above): *Beach, Point Reyes, CA,* 2005. A grab shot with a pocket camera on an exursion with my daughter. The pine and the cloud above it are in perfect harmony.

Page 9 (Below): *The Church of St. Francis of Assisi, Taos, NM,* 1985. Full polarization with a 28mm Nikor, the only focal length possible in the cramped square, shot at *f* 32 for 1/4 sec., with full polarization and a neutral density filter.

Page 10 (Above): *Street, Truchas, NM,* 1985. Shot at 1/15 sec. to capture the movement of the wind, and a polarizer and neutral density filter to lower the f-stop to 32.

Page 10 (Below): *Blue Nude,* 1976. Photographed in Greenbrook Nature Sanctuary in Tenafly, New Jersey, a wonderful photographic resource for me for many years, on Ektachrome Tungsten film only partially corrected for outdoor use to bring out that lovely shade of blue and emphasize, I think, the yummy curves.

Page 11: *Indian Water, Taos Pueblo, Taos, NM*, 1985. Shot at 1/30th sec. with partial polarization. I was unaware that this stream is thought of as sacred by the Navajo and was startled when a member of the tribe came screaming at me while I was packing up my tripod. It prints even better at larger scale.

Page 12: *Staircase, Grey Towers, Milford, PA*, 2010. Completely unmanipulated, though some people swear it must be a montage.

Page 13 (Above): *Study in Primary Colors, Bovina Center, NY*, 2006. The subject was a banged-up kid's scooter model. Shot RAW at $f4$ in a drizzle in front of a locavore restaurant in town. It would have been a crisper image if I'd had my tripod, but it's amazing what correct breathing can do.

Page 13 (Below): *Green Pepper*, 1977. I had been looking at a lot of Edward Weston nudes when I took this series. The form swept me away. Shot at $f32$ on Kodachrome 25 with no filtration.

Page 14: *Beach Fence, Soffit, Cloud, Misquamicut Beach, RI*, 2009. Shot with a 60mm Nikkor and polarizing filter. The composition *looks* common enough, but try finding one like it!

Page 15: *Tomato*, 1976. A 55mm Macro-Nikkor image on Kodachrome 64, minus some distracting surface dust. If I had to take three of my photographs with me to a desert island, this would be one of them.

Page 16 (Above): *Cream Dahlia, Stonecrop Gardens*, 2009. Stonecrop Gardens, in Cold Spring, New York, has been a constant source of inspiration for me. Taken at $f32$ with a 60mm Macro-Nikkor under high overcast.

Page 16 (Below): *Dawn, Provincetown, MA*, 1974. Shot at $f22$ with a 35mm Nikkor lens, long exposure; Thoreau said that the triangle is the strongest form in Nature.

Page 17 (Above): *Water Study, Beacon, NY*, 2006. Shot at the dam in Beacon, a wonderful place to make pictures. Shot at 1/15 sec. with an 80-200mm Nikkor and full polarization.

Page 17 (Below): *Pink Rose, Stonecrop Gardens*, 2009. It still takes my breath away. $f5.6$ under a pearly sky with an 80mm Macro Nikkor.

Page 18: *Geometry, Beacon, NY*, 2008. There is absolutely no manipulation in this image, much influenced I think by many years of studying Japanese art. Shot at 1/30 sec. with partial polarization.

Page 19: *Gray's Beach and Sky, Yarmouthport, MA*, 2006. One of the most beautiful places I have ever seen.

Page 20: *Low Tide, Hudson River*, 1991. Shot not far from my apartment building after a period of snow that left the air moist and shadowless. Getting the tripod in place was difficult— only the bright edge of the central rock was above water. Shot at $f32$, 1 sec. exposure, with a 50mm Nikkor. The composition makes this a personal favorite.

Page 21: *Dawn, Centerville, MA*, 1993. My dear friend Howard Pollack and I were out early one morning and found this waiting for us. It took a while for the geese to join us. Shot at *f* 32 for1/2 sec. on Kodachrome 64.

Page 22: *African Mask,* 1993. Shot at *f* 16 for 1/10 sec on Kodachrome 64.

Page 23: *Marsh Grasses, Centerville, MA,* 1993.

Page 24 (Above): *Hudson River, Tallman Mountain,* 2007. Slight polarization, tightly framed.

Page 24 (Below): *Clouds, Key West, FL,* 1976. Shot from Mallory Pier at sunset, at *f* 32 with full polarization, in the days when Mallory Pier Sunset was a very laid-back, mostly underpopulated experience.

Page 25 (Above): *Pond, Stonecrop Gardens, Carmel, NY,* 2009. I was enchanted by the Impressionistic quality of this moment. Partial polarization with a 200mm Nikkor zoom.

Page 25 (Below): *Waterfall, Beacon, NY,* 2006. This startling image was the first in a series I have made of the falls—shot at 1000 sec. with partial polarization on a Nikkor zoom set at 170mm.

Page 26: *Tinsel, Bovina, NY,* 2006. Shot in slanting late afternoon light with an 80mm Micro-Nikkor, polarized and unmanipulated.

Page 27: *Streetlight, La Boca, Buenos Aires,* 2007. These are true colors; shot with partial polarization.

Page 28 (Above): *Lotus, Stonecrop Gardens, Carmel, NY,* 2006.

Page 28 (Below): *White Rose,* 1976. Studies like this one, shot on Kodachrome 25 with a 55mm Micro-Nikkor, reflect my earliest investigations of organic form, which is, as Edward Weston put it, "the strongest way of seeing a shape."

Page 29 (Above): *Yellow Rose,* 1975. Another macro image, intentionally overexposed on Kodachrome 25 to create an ethereal sense of movement; Peter Fink, the great *Vogue* photographer, told me he was much taken by its airy *ingenue* feeling.

Page 29 (Below): *Marriage,* 2009. I prefer to avoid metaphoric titles for photographs; occasionally, one expresses what I was trying to say before I released the shutter. This was shot in indirect indoor light with an 80mm Micro-Nikkor.

Page 30: *Seawall (Horse Form), Truro, MA,* 1997. Forty years ago, I found a seawall, constructed of pilings behind the tennis court at Pamet Harbor, that had faced rising and falling tides for perhaps a century. I have returned to it again and again. Dead low tide on an overcast day; shot at *f* 32, long exposure for 1 sec. with an 80mm Micro-Nikkor.

Page 31: *Seawall (Owl Form), Truro, MA,* 1997.

Page 32: *Seawall (Cliff Form), Truro, MA,* 1997.

Page 33: *David's Flower, 1977.* This is the same subject as the images on pages 36–37—a giant magnolia, photographed here on Ektachrome Indoor film with a 55mm Micro-Nikkor, at *f* 32 and long exposure, under *completely* corrected tungsten light.

Page 34: *The Gateless Gate, Peggy Mills Gardens, Key West, FL,* 1977. The place, like perhaps too much of Key West, is long gone. The palette absolutely enthralled me.

Page 35: *Black Buddha, Jacques Marchais Museum, Staten Island*, 2006. This image shares with the previous one the way nature alters the manmade, a boundary that has always informed my eye.

Page 36: *Giant Magnolia, Prayer Form*, 1977. This image, the next, and the one on Page 56 were all shot with *partial* correction for tungsten light. The image on page 33 is of the same subject.

Page 37: *Giant Magnolia, Vase Form*, 1977.

Page 38: *Sunset, Pamet Harbor, Truro, MA*, 1974. Shot on Kodak Infra-Red film with an ASA assignment of 200 and an orange filter. It was difficult to make images on that emulsion that were warm. This was a happy calculation; a client who lived at Pamet Harbor once told me that this photograph was warmer than the actual place.

Page 39: *Bridge Detail, Centerville, MA*, 1997. I wonder if the folks who hammered these two-by-fours together realized how visually powerful a creation they had wrought. Shot at f4.

Page 40 (Above): *Study in Blue, Black, and White*, 2006. Shot digitally with a a Nikkor Zoom ar 200mm, full polarization.

Page 40 (Below): *Gummybears, Rome*, 2002. Breathing correctly is a key factor in making photographs: This was shot at 1/25 sec. because I wanted maximal depth of field, but I don't think you can tell.

Page 41 (Above): *Barn Window, Milford, PA*, 2010. I like the weathering of the window as much as of the siding.

Page 41 (Below): *Trapped Leaf, Beacon, NY*, 2006. Shot at 200mm with moderate polarization.

Page 42: *Flag and Yellow Porch, Cold Spring, NY*, 2007. The shady light here was extraordinary; the image suggests an America long gone.

Page 43: *Wild Orchid, Coral Gables, FL*, 1976. I see all sorts of energies in flowers; this one was particularly explosive.

Page 44: *Tulip*, 1977. Shot with a Macro lens on Kodachrome 25 in wonderful pale light.

Page 45: *Pumpkin*, 1975. I saw the Romanesque groining in this from the first; do you?

Page 46: *Study in Grays, Mystic, CT*, 2006. I was after the sense of tranquillity in this image, which draws the eye to the vase in the background.

Page 47: *Dead Tide, Effect of Light, Yarmouthport, MA*, 2006. This was, of course, exposed for the white stern of the sailing craft. The entire composition depends on it. Full polarization.

Page 48: *Construction Site, Beacon, NY*, 2006. This, and the image on the facing page, share a common theme.

Page 49: *Moss and water, Greenbrook Nature Sanctuary, Tenafly, NJ*, 2006.

Page 50 (Above): *Red Rose I*, 1975. Another Macro image shot at f32. Great thighs.

Page 50 (Below): *Seawall (Nodal Form), Truro, MA*, 1997.

Page 51 (Above): *Door, Key West,* 1995. I am a sucker for weathering. As Loren Eiseley once put it re the High Plains during the Dust Bowl years in the 1930s, "The soft stuff goes first, / And that includes Man."

Page 51 (Below): *Party Decoration, Centerville, MA,* 1993.

Page 52: *Red Rose II,* 1975. The same subject as on Page 50 (Above), but with a very different feeling.

Page 53: *Red Cabbage, 1977.* I draped a leaf of the cabbage over the lens, with extension tube, to produce this at maximal depth of field with tricky manual focus. The image also appears on the cover.

Page 54: *Barns, Truchas, NM*, 1985. A most magical place, one of the few I have ever been in where there were photographs anywhere I looked.

Page 55: *Boardwalk Detail, Grey's Beach, Yarmouthport, MA,* 1997. The delicious depth of the water revealed by polarization contrasts perfectly, I thought, with the severe geometry of the structure.

Page 56 (Above): *Pansy,* 1977. Another macro shot, done 1:1 at f32 with an extension tube.

Page 56 (Below): *Giant Magnolia, Nodal Form,* 1977.

Page 57: *Flight,* 1977.

www.ingramcontent.com/pod-product-compliance
Lightning Source LLC
Chambersburg PA
CBHW050743180526
45159CB00003B/1333